Received On:

JUN 2 2 2013

Ballard Branch

D0803517

THIS IS NO LONGER THE PROPERTY

OF THE SEATTLE PUBLIC LIBRARY

curriculum
connections

Psychology

The History of Psychology

BROWN
BEAR
BOOKS

Published by Brown Bear Books Limited

4877 N. Circulo Bujia
Tucson
AZ 85718
USA

First Floor
9–17 St. Albans Place
London N1 0NX
UK

www.brownreference.com

© 2010 The Brown Reference Group Ltd

ISBN: 978-1-936333-15-8

All right reserved. This book is protected by copyright. No part of it may be reproduced, stored in a retrieval system, or transmitted in any form or by any means, without the prior permission in writing of the Publisher, nor be otherwise circulated in any form of binding or cover other than that in which it is published and without a similar condition including this condition being imposed on the subsequent publisher.

Editorial Director: Lindsey Lowe
Managing Editor: Tim Cooke
Project Director: Laura Durman
Editor: Helen Dwyer
Designer: Barry Dwyer
Picture Researcher: Barry Dwyer

Library of Congress Cataloging-in-Publication Data available upon request

Picture Credits

Cover Image
Thinkstock: istockphoto.

iStockphoto: p. 37 (Brad Killer); Shutterstock: pp. 16 (posztos/colorlab.hu), 18 (feverpitch), 21 (Ewen Cameron), 23 (Renata Osinska), 27 (Blamb), 29 (Keith Gentry), 41 (Ruta Saulyte-Laurinaviciene), 45 (Castka), 51 (BestPhoto1), 55 (argo74), 57 (Africa Studio), 58 (Pixel Memoirs), 68 (Daniela Sachsenheimer), 71 (Bojan Pavlukovic), 74 (Martin Novak), 81 (Wolfgang Amri), 85 (Studio 1One), 92 (Epic Stock), 95 (zulufoto), 97 (Muellek Josef), 101 (doglikehorse); Wikimedia Commons: pp. 12, 38 (Ferdinand Schmutzer), 47 (Harke), 102 (Devriese)

Artwork © The Brown Reference Group Ltd

The Brown Reference Group Ltd has made every effort to trace copyright holders of the pictures used in this book. Anyone having claims to ownership not identified above is invited to contact The Brown Reference Group Ltd.

Printed in the United States of America

Contents

Introduction

Psychology forms part of the Curriculum Connections series. Each of the six volumes of the set covers a particular aspect of psychology: History of Psychology; The Brain; Cognitive Development; Intellectual Development; The Individual and Society; and Abnormal Psychology.

About this set

Each volume in *Psychology* features illustrated chapters, providing in-depth information about each subject. The chapters are all listed in the contents pages of each book. Each volume can be studied to provide a comprehensive understanding of the different aspects of psychology. However, each chapter may also be studied independently.

Within each chapter there are two key aids to learning that are to be found in color sidebars located in the margins of each page:

Curriculum Context sidebars indicate to the reader that a subject has a particular relevance to certain key state and national psychology guidelines and curricula. They highlight essential information or suggest useful ways for students to consider a subject or to include it in their studies.

Glossary sidebars define key words within the text.

At the end of the book, a summary **Glossary** lists the key terms defined in the volume. There is also a list of further print and Web-based resources and a full volume index.

Fully captioned illustrations play an important role throughout the set, including photographs and explanatory diagrams.

About this book

History of Psychology provides the historical context that will help readers to better understand the richness and complexity of psychology, the science of mind and behavior.

Starting in Ancient Greece, this volume examines the earliest concepts of "mind" as well as the changing attitudes toward mental illness through history. It explores psychology's roots in both philosophy and natural science, from the theories of key figures, such as Aristotle and Hippocrates, to studies of Western scholars in the Middle Ages, through to Francis Galton's application of evolutionary principles to people.

The volume goes on to examine the scientific research of the nineteenth century, notably the work of Gustav Fechner, Hermann Helmholtz, and Wilhelm Wundt. It describes the emergence of experimental psychology and the impact that it had on empirical methods.

The volume then charts the development of diverse psychological theories throughout the 20th century, from Gestalt psychology, psychoanalysis, and behaviorism through to cognitive psychology. It also examines the development of recent approaches, such as evolutionary psychology, and considers the effects of new research in nonwestern cultures.

Ancient Greek Thought

In the Western world the earliest evidence of a systematic exploration of the idea of the mind dates back to ancient Greece. For Greek philosophers and physicians the key issues were the basic nature of the mind (what it was made of) and its various functions and parts.

Curriculum Context

You may be expected to compare philosophical psychology to more modern forms of psychology.

Cosmos

The universe seen as a well-ordered whole.

Thumos

The cause of courage, indignation, anger, and other action-oriented emotional states.

Before the 19th century psychology was considered part of philosophy. The earliest known Greek philosophers tackled two of the key questions of the time: identifying the basic element of the world and finding out why the universe moved on its own. They all believed that the universe had a *psyche*—the force that caused things to change.

Metempsychosis

Pythagoras (about 570–500 B.C.) established a school in Italy. None of his writings survive but his pupils believed that all things could be reduced to numerical relationships—even abstract ideas such as justice were associated with a number. This focus on number and proportion led to a belief in the harmony of the cosmos. The Pythagoreans also believed that the psyche passed at death from one body to the next—human or animal—in an endless series of lives, a doctrine known as metempsychosis (or reincarnation).

Heraclitus

Heraclitus (about 540–480 B.C.) believed that the essence of all things was formed by an underlying structure. This underlying structure governing the organization of the cosmos was called *logos*, which translates as "plan," "reason," or "word."

Heraclitus thought that the psyche was a mysterious object that one could never know fully. Psyche and *thumos* (strong emotion) were opposites.

The cosmos

Anaxagoras of Clazomenae (about 500–428 B.C.) developed a theory about *nous* (rationality, or intellect). He expanded the meaning of the term to include the rationality of the cosmos as a whole— the principle that kept the world orderly.

Empedocles of Acragas (about 492–432 B.C.) said that the cosmos was composed of four elements: fire, air, earth, and water. He claimed that all material objects continually gave off tiny copies of themselves, and that these were picked up by the sense organs and transmitted to the heart.

Democritus of Abdera (born about 460 B.C.) believed that all things were made of tiny, indivisible atoms. The smallest and smoothest atoms were in the psyche, which explained the speed of perception and thought.

Socrates

When Athens lost a long war it went into decline. During this period Socrates (about 470–399 B.C.) would roam the marketplace, engaging people in debate about the nature of virtue, truth, justice, and goodness. A small group of young men gathered about him to learn. In 399 B.C. Socrates was put on public trial for "impiety" and "corrupting" the young men of Athens. He was forced to kill himself by drinking poison.

Plato's theory of the psyche

One of Socrates' followers was Plato (about 428–348 B.C.). In his early works he wrote about the possibility of improving one's psyche through learning and of the psyche being the source of human morality. Later he declared that the psyche was in command of the body, being the seat of all knowledge. Knowledge was inborn and experience brought this knowledge to consciousness, through a process of recollection (*anamnesis*). Plato also said that the psyche was

Rationality
The quality of being based on reason or logic.

Perception
The process by which one becomes aware of external stimuli.

Curriculum Context

Students may be asked to examine the influence of the theories of Plato and other Greek philosophers on later Western studies of the mind.

Platonic Forms

How do we come to know things? How do we know, for example, that a horse is a horse? Plato believed that all horses have something in common that enables us to identify them as horses. This something is not their similarity in appearance, because they appear in many different colors, shapes, and sizes. Plato believed that there must be an "Idea of Horse" that all horses "reflect." The same went for abstract ideas such as virtue and justice—all just acts are just because they reflect the Idea of Justice. These Ideas are known as Platonic "Forms."

Plato argued that the things around us are like distorted shadows of the true Forms. In order to know the Forms, we cannot depend on just looking straight ahead. Instead, we have to explore further by thinking about the essence of each thing.

immortal, and that the death of the body freed the psyche to be with the Forms that one could only glimpse, via philosophy, for as long as the psyche is trapped in the body.

In *Republic* Plato argued that the psyche was made of three distinct parts: the *logistikon* (the intellect); the *thumos* (the emotions); and the *epithumetikon*. In the best psyche the *logistikon* ruled, harmonizing the needs of the three parts through the use of reason.

Epithumetikon

In Ancient Greek philosophy, the seat of appetites and desires.

Aristotle

Aristotle (384–322 B.C.) was a student of Plato. In his book *On the Soul* Aristotle considers how the psyche and the body combine to produce a living being. Aristotle believed that the psyche was the form (or the organization) given to the matter of the body. Together, psyche and body made the living thing.

Aristotle said that the psyche has five faculties: nutrition (basic to life), perception, desire, locomotion, and intellect. Nutrition was basic to life and was the only faculty plants had. To be an animal, a living thing had to have the faculty of perception: sight, touch, taste, smell, and hearing. If an animal had perception, it also had imagination and desire. Aristotle attributed locomotion only to some animals. Finally, he considered just a few animals to have intellect.

Greek medical tradition

Followers of the medical tradition of ancient Greece also had much to say about the mind, sometimes in opposition to the philosophers. Hippocrates of Kos (about 460–377 B.C.) and his disciples show a preference for observation over abstract reason and for concrete explanations rather than metaphysical (supernatural) ones.

In many medical writings health was related to a balance between competing or opposing elements, such as hot and cold. It was also considered important to maintain the correct balance between the four bodily fluids called the humors: blood, phlegm, yellow bile, and black bile. Imbalances were thought to cause specific diseases and mental problems. This doctrine of the humors formed the basis of medical care well into the Middle Ages.

Phlegm
The secretions of the mucous membranes of the respiratory passages.

Bile
A bitter fluid that is secreted by the liver and aids digestion.

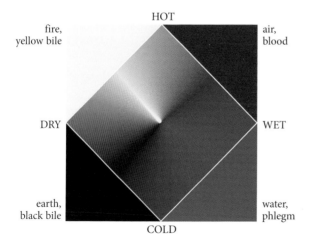

Medical theory in ancient Greece was based on maintaining a balance between opposites and the four humors. Each of the humors, or bodily fluids, was related to one of the four basic elements (earth, fire, water, and air).

Early Psychology

Today psychology is the study of behavior and mental processes, while psychiatry is a branch of medicine concerned with the treatment of mental illnesses. Originally, however, they were both seen as branches of philosophy.

The word psychology comes from two Greek words: *psyche*, meaning "mind" or "soul," and *logos*, meaning "word" or "reason." The word psychiatry, also Greek in origin, comes from *psyche* and *iatros*, meaning "to heal."

The Greek physician–philosopher Hippocrates proposed that illnesses were caused by an imbalance of body fluids, or humors: blood, phlegm, yellow bile, and black bile. Madness was thought to be caused by an excess of black bile (*melan chole* in Greek). Later, Greek practitioners advocated quiet, useful occupation, and drugs as remedies for mental illness.

The Middle Ages

During the Middle Ages (about the 5th to 15th centuries) Western scholars studied human behavior from a religious viewpoint. People who were seen to behave unusually were thought to be possessed by evil spirits or influenced by witchcraft, and sufferers were usually considered to have sinned in some way. Treatments aimed at releasing these evil spirits, and the sweat house was a building where a smoldering fire smoked out demons and "treated" those afflicted. While some sufferers were cared for by religious orders, many were forced to become beggars and vagrants.

Religious order
A society of monks, priests, or nuns following particular religious and social disciplines.

The birth of psychology

Between the 14th and 17th centuries studies of the mind and brain anatomy were revitalized. Instead of studying animals, thinkers turned their attention to human behavior and anatomy. The term psychology was first used in 1506.

Anatomy
The study of the bodily structure of living organisms.

The French philosopher René Descartes (1596–1650) suggested that the body and the mind (or rational soul) were separate structures that strongly influenced each other. The rational soul interacted with the body through the brain and was the seat of wisdom. The Dutch philosopher Baruch Spinoza (1632–1677) believed that mind and body coordinated their actions because they were influenced by the same stimuli.

Pseudoscience

During the Middle Ages people with mental illness were thought to have *stigmata diaboli* (marks of the devil). Supposedly they were physical marks, but the interpretation of what one looked like was greatly subjective. Many people found to have these marks were subsequently executed. By the 19th century stigmata were being used as a way of diagnosing mental illness.

Swiss theologian Johann Kaspar Lavater (1741–1801) first advocated the use of facial expressions to diagnose mental illness. This technique was also used to detect criminals. Guillaume Duchenne (1806–1875), a French neurologist, created a complete book of facial expressions with photographs of different kinds of "looks" and descriptions of what they denoted.

Madhouses

In Europe from the 17th century onward many people who were seen as being outside normal society were confined together in institutions called madhouses. This included people who were mentally ill or handicapped and those who were criminals and vagrants. Madhouses were like prisons. Physicians sometimes visited to purge the inmates with herbal tonics, but many of the people there were shackled, chained to walls, or put in straitjackets.

Purge
Treat by causing vomiting or evacuation of the bowels.

In 1793 French physician Philippe Pinel (1745–1826) was given responsibility for an institution for mentally ill men in Paris, France. Disgusted at the inhumane treatment of the inmates, Pinel demanded that they be unshackled, given pleasant rooms, and allowed to exercise in the grounds. Pinel categorized insanity into

Insanity
The state of being seriously mentally ill; madness.

The oldest and most famous madhouse, the Hospital of St. Mary of Bethlehem in London, England, was a horrific place of cruelty, neglect, whips, chains, and filth. *Bethlehem* was shortened to *Bethlem* or *Bedlam*, a word that came to mean "uproar."

melancholia, mania, idiocy, and dementia, and partial insanity. He did away with treatments like purging and bleeding in favor of discussions with the patient and a program of activities.

The Tukes

In 1796 a Quaker community in England built a charitable retreat based on quiet, comfort, and a supportive atmosphere. The Tukes family ran the institution, paving the way for widespread changes in attitude. With the success of the Tukes' efforts the notion that mental illness was a medical condition requiring skilled treatment began to gain acceptance.

Science and humanity

As a result of changing attitudes to mental illness, madhouses were renamed asylums during the early 1800s. The idea was emerging that mental illness originated within the person, possibly in the brain. There was a sharp rise in the number of books on mental disorders and in the number of practicing physicians, who were known as mad-doctors. By the 1850s interest in the nature and treatment of mental illness was growing, and there was widespread optimism that it might be curable.

Curriculum Context

It may be interesting to compare changing attitudes to mental illness with new attitudes toward other groups, such as the sick or the poor, in the 19th century.

Science and psychology

Psychology and psychiatry remained closely linked until the mid 19th century, when German scientists began examining mental activity using scientific methods of observation. Wilhelm Wundt (1832–1920), published a journal of experimental psychology, establishing psychology as a distinct discipline based on careful observation. These scientists helped separate psychology from philosophy and from psychiatry, which was developing its own identity.

Psychoanalysis

One approach in psychiatry is psychoanalysis, developed by Sigmund Freud (1856–1939). Originally a therapeutic strategy, it is also a theory of mental disorder and an approach to understanding human nature. Freud believed that forces buried deep in the subconscious mind determined behavior, and that repressed feelings caused personality disturbances, self-destructive tendencies, and physical problems.

Crossover and interaction

Today psychology and psychiatry are separate disciplines. Psychologists study normal and abnormal behavior, typically obtaining an academic degree and then moving on to further specialized training. Psychiatry is a medical speciality: Psychiatrists specialize in disorders of the mind and brain and have earned a medical degree. They are also licensed to prescribe and administer drugs and therapies.

There are still many areas of crossover, however. In 1879 the term "clinical psychology" was introduced to describe analysis carried out in a clinical setting such as a hospital, and clinical psychologists who work as therapists in mental health centers often train under experienced psychiatrists. Psychologists and psychiatrists will also cooperate to help their patients cope with all kinds of problems and mental illnesses.

Subconscious

Concerning the part of the mind that influences actions and feelings, but that one is not fully aware of.

Curriculum Context

Students may be expected to understand the differences and similarities between psychology and other social sciences, such as psychiatry.

Nature and Nurture

The "nature–nurture debate" concerns a fundamental question about psychology: To what extent is the human mind a product of nature, or biology, and to what extent is it a result of nurture, or experience? People have pondered this issue ever since they began to think about the mind.

Early history

The debate can be traced at least as far back as the fourth century B.C. to the Greek philosopher Aristotle, who compared the mind to a blank slate to be written on by impressions from the senses. This view persisted through the Middle Ages.

In the 16th century an English schoolmaster Richard Mulcaster (about 1513–1611) introduced the terms "nature" and "nurture" to refer to the poles of the debate. He suggested that both biology and experience were important in a child's development.

The pendulum swings

With the publication of Charles Darwin's *On the Origin of Species* in 1859, biology began to play a broader role in the nature–nurture debate. The English scientist Francis Galton (1822–1911) applied the principles of evolution to people. He focused on the question of which force, nature or nurture, was responsible for generating differences between individuals.

Galton reasoned that there were only two sources that could generate differences between people: different biological features inherited from parents and different environmental forces, including peoples' experiences and learning. He further reasoned that researchers could investigate the influence of heredity by looking at how traits ran in families. He argued that superior mental capacity could be inherited.

Evolution

The process by which different organisms are thought to have developed, over time, from earlier forms.

Heredity

The passing on of physical or mental characteristics from generation to generation.

The rise of behaviorism

At the same time, another school of psychology was emerging—behaviorism. The father of behaviorism—U.S. psychologist John B. Watson (1878–1958)—put the emphasis on experience. Behaviorism sought to explain behavior in terms of two laws of learning: classical conditioning and operant conditioning.

Physiologist Ivan Pavlov (1849–1936) discovered classical conditioning by accident. He was studying dogs' digestive processes when he noticed something peculiar: While he was in the process of delivering food to the dogs, they would begin to salivate even before the food had arrived. He discovered that, by ringing a bell just before feeding time, he could condition the dogs to salivate when they heard the sound. They had formed a link between the sound and the food.

Psychologist E. L. Thorndike (1874–1949) contributed to a different theory of learning called operant conditioning. He suggested that animals tended to repeat actions that produced a positive result. Behaviors that were rewarded were repeated, while behaviors that were punished were not. Psychologist B. F. Skinner (1904–1990) extended Thorndike's work. In Skinner's experiments animals were rewarded for engaging in certain behaviors that the researcher was trying to encourage.

These theories emphasized experience as the source of behavior. They suggested that biology's contribution was merely an innate sense of what was rewarding.

The decline of behaviorism

Opponents of behaviorist theory believed that animals were more than blank slates. They thought that if they could show that animals formed some associations more easily than others, it would suggest that more was innate than merely the ability to learn associations.

Classical conditioning

Training a person or an animal to behave in a certain way in response to an unrelated stimulus.

Operant conditioning

Training a person or an animal to behave in a certain way by punishment or reward.

Salivate

To secrete saliva, a watery liquid that aids chewing, swallowing, and digestion.

Biological Approaches and Politics

In the late 19th and early 20th centuries, a growing emphasis on nature rather than nurture gave birth to three movements that had serious political consequences: social Darwinism, biological determinism, and eugenics.

Social Darwinists held that social groups were subject to the forces of natural selection in the same way that individuals were under Darwin's theory—that is, they believed that stronger groups of individuals would eventually outcompete and replace weaker groups of individuals. They applied this idea to all kinds of groups, including nations, races, and ethnicities.

In the political arena social Darwinism was used to justify the oppression of particular groups, such as the poor or minorities. In economics business leaders used the idea to support the notion that governments should not intervene in business, arguing that allowing firms to compete freely enabled the best firms to survive.

Biological determinism, also known as genetic determinism, was the idea that genes alone determined a person's fate. In other words, an organism would develop in the same way regardless of the environment in which it was placed. Some politicians in the 1920s and early 1930s used this argument to justify reduced government spending in areas such as welfare and education. If destiny was determined by genes, the genetic determinists argued then, no amount of spending would have any improving effect on the lives of the poor.

Eugenics was the idea that people could improve the genetic quality of the human race by controlling who was allowed to reproduce. Eugenicists believed that only members of "superior" social groups should be permitted to have children: In this way the human race would gradually improve. These arguments were vehemently rejected when the Nazis used them to justify genocide (mass murder).

The Nazi leader, Adolf Hitler, was an enthusiastic supporter of eugenics, which he saw as a way of eliminating Jews, black people, and homosexuals. This is Auschwitz, one of the concentration camps where thousands of Jews were murdered.

Scientist John Garcia (born 1917) and his colleagues conducted a series of experiments with rats in the mid-1960s. Garcia gave his rats a little tube to drink from, which dispensed a solution with a distinctive flavor that the rats had never tasted before. Whenever the rats drank from the tube, a light came on, and there was a little "click" sound. Each time this happened, the rats were exposed to X-rays that made them temporarily ill.

If the behaviorists were correct, the rats should have come to associate all three conditions—the light, the click, and the taste of the solution—with feeling sick. They should have learned to avoid all three. Instead, the rats learned to avoid the solution, but not the light or the click, suggesting that they associated being sick with the novel taste, not with the light or the sound.

This was exactly what Garcia expected to find. Rats in their natural environments need to learn which foods are good to eat and which are poisonous. To do this, they learn to avoid any new food that makes them sick.

Curriculum Context

Students who are studying behaviorism might wish to consider other experiments that could be used to test the theories.

Misbehavior

At around the same time Keller and Marian Breland published a paper entitled "The Misbehavior of Organisms," giving numerous examples of experiments in which the organisms being studied did not behave as behaviorist theory predicted.

In the 1950s and 1960s evidence against behaviorism continued to accumulate. Wolfgang Köhler (1887–1967) showed that chimpanzees did not need their behavior reinforced or rewarded to solve some problems. Instead, they could use "insight," working out the solution by careful perception of the problem.

Harry Harlow (1905–1981) separated newborn monkeys from their natural mothers and provided them with an artificial "mother" made from hard, uncomfortable wire but equipped with a feeding tube and nipple. Despite being rewarded by this "mother," the monkeys did not become attached to it. In contrast, a doll made of soft, fluffy material proved rewarding because it was comforting to touch and hold.

The cognitive revolution

In the late 1950s the linguist Noam Chomsky claimed that humans had a language "organ": a distinct part of the brain specifically for learning language. According to Chomsky, the ability to learn a language was innate. Chomsky also argued that there are certain properties that all languages have in common. The similarities were a result of the innate language organ (the areas of the brain that produced speech) that all people shared. This organ was only capable of learning languages with certain grammatical rules, so all world's languages were constructed from the same set of possible rules.

Chomsky's work marked the start of the cognitive revolution. Cognitive psychologists viewed the mind as a machine that took in information from the world, processed it, and then generated behavior. Chomsky had also argued that there were innate learning mechanisms in people's heads that enabled them to learn about the world. Thus cognitive psychologists sought to describe other innate learning mechanisms.

Linguist

Someone who studies languages and their structure.

Cognitive psychologists try to understand which structures in the brain enable people to learn about the world around them. For example, the work of linguist Noam Chomsky showed that people are born with the capacity to learn language, but that their environment is responsible for the specific language that they learn.

Sociobiology

With the cognitive revolution, nativism once again became respectable. In 1975 Edward O. Wilson published a book entitled *Sociobiology*. In it Wilson proposed that the social behavior of all animals, including people, was based on genetics. Others also tried to use biology as a way of understanding human psychology. In 1979 Donald Symons published *The Evolution of Human Sexuality*, a look at how evolution by natural selection might have shaped human sexual behavior.

During the 1980s and 1990s evolutionary psychology emerged. It took many ideas from sociobiology and cognitive science. Evolutionary psychologists saw evolution as a force that built information-processing systems, enabling each organism to interact adaptively with its environment. Genes (inherited codes) constructed the organism jointly, together with the environment.

In his book *The Language Instinct* (1994), psychologist Steven Pinker referred to the language organ as an instinct, calling attention to the way in which natural selection built information-processing systems that enabled people to learn new ideas. Accumulating more and more information-processing systems through natural selection made people increasingly flexible.

Untangling the debate

After ample research, it now seems likely that there is no absolute answer to the nature–nurture debate. Every aspect of an individual is thought to be the product of both genes and the environment. It is also thought to be impossible to divide a person's traits into "environmental" and "genetic" components because every organism's genes interact with the environment in a complex way to build that organism.

Nativism
The belief that mental concepts and structures are present from birth rather than learned later.

Genetics
The process by which the properties or features of an organism are transmitted to its offspring.

Cognitive science
Studies of the human mind and how it works.

Beginnings of Scientific Psychology

In the 18th and 19th centuries developments in sciences such as chemistry and physics led to the emergence of psychology as a scientific discipline. One of the scientists influenced by these advances was Wilhelm Wundt (1832–1920), who introduced introspection as a research tool for the study of the mind.

Physiology
The study of the way living organisms and their body parts work.

Psychophysics
The application of the principles of physics to mental processes.

There were huge advances in science during the 18th and 19th centuries, especially in the fields of physiology (how bodies work), physics, and chemistry. As effective experimental techniques developed, many of the latest scientific theories were published and applied to technology and contemporary life. Science, scientists, experimentation, and the laboratory became fascinating to many people. The new emphasis on science meant that people began to view psychology in a different light.

Fechner and Helmholtz
Gustav Fechner (1801–1887) was the founder of the field of "psychophysics". Fechner used mathematics and physics to understand the mind, quantifying the mathematical relationship between different levels of stimuli and the mind's perception of them. For example, Fechner conducted research in which various levels of sound intensities were presented to volunteers; their reaction times were measured as they attempted to indicate when they first heard each stimulus. Fechner discovered distinct patterns, one of which he called the auditory perceptual threshold: that is, the average minimum intensity necessary for people to hear a sound.

Hermann Helmholtz (1821–1894) developed a theory of color perception, which had initially been proposed by Thomas Young (1773–1829) in 1801. This theory (ultimately called the Young–Helmholtz three-color theory) still helps explain many of the facts of color perception, especially the way in which cells in the retina of the eye process colors.

Helmholtz was also interested in the speed of neural (nerve) impulses. He conducted empirical research using motor nerves (which impart motion) in frogs. He found that the speed of the neural impulse was 90 ft. (19m) per second.

Empirical
Based on observation or experience rather than on theory or logic.

Helmholtz wanted to understand how sensory information was processed by the brain: in other words, how external stimuli such as light and vibrations made their way into people's minds as sight and sound. One of his main conclusions was that these sensations from the external world only made sense in the brain after being organized in a logical way.

Phrenology

Phrenology became popular in the 19th century. It appeared to use scientific techniques but has been wholly discredited by later research, although it enjoyed great popular appeal.

Phrenology was based on the idea that all mental faculties were located in specific regions of the brain. These regions influenced the shape of the skull, which meant that mental abilities and character traits could be determined by studying the shape of the skull. For example, if a person had a good memory, the area of the brain responsible for the function of memory would be enlarged, and that would be noticeable on the

person's skull. Phrenologists drew detailed diagrams of the brain on models of the skull, labeling the structures and their functions.

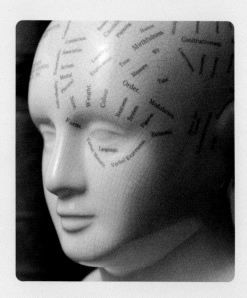

This phrenological head is based on Franz Josef Gall's map of the 26 principal "organs," or faculties. Other phrenology enthusiasts made several adaptations.

Animal and human psychology

In 1862 Wilhelm Wundt gave a series of lectures on animal and human psychology at the University of Heidelberg. It was the first course ever taught in scientific psychology, and it firmly separated psychology from physiology and philosophy for the first time. Wundt taught that psychology should be experimental and scientific. He believed that many psychological phenomena, such as perception and sensation, were measurable. However, he suggested that psychology had limitations because it could not explain complex human functioning, such as higher mental processing or social interaction.

Wundt believed that human behavior resulted from a complex interaction between motivations and other subtle, often unknown influences. He said that these elements could not be measured because none of them directly caused behavior on their own. Wundt stated that human behavior was not measurable in the same way that physical phenomena were measurable.

This position marked a clear separation of psychology from physiology, physics, and chemistry. Today most psychologists disagree with Wundt's views. They believe that psychology is a rigorous science.

Introspection

Psychophysiology investigates how people and nonhuman animals sense the external world and how they perceive information from sensory data, and today it is considered a branch of psychology.

Wundt developed systematic methods to measure the basic elements of sensation and perception. The science of physics relied on techniques of inspection (observation) to study physical phenomena; Wundt sought to develop introspection to study people's mental phenomena.

Phenomenon

(plural: phenomena)
An observable fact, condition, or event.

Curriculum Context

Curricula may ask students to identify Wundt's contributions to experimental psychology.

Introspection

The examination of one's own mental and emotional processes.

Psychophysiologists accept that the senses, such as vision, smell, and taste, send sensory information to the brain, where the process of perception occurs; but they try to determine how much of what we know is due to the sense organs themselves, and how much is due to the brain and its perceptual processing.

The subjects in these experiments were called observers, and they were trained to report their thoughts and feelings. They would be presented with a stimulus, such as a shape or color, and had to report their thoughts in response to that stimulus. The difficult part was that they were supposed to separate their knowledge from their memories of the stimulus object, so that they could give an objective report of their immediate thoughts and feelings.

Objective
Not influenced by personal feelings or opinions.

Flaws in introspection

Introspection proved to have flaws as a scientific method. By its very nature it was unverifiable, because there was no way to determine whether the observers were reporting their true thoughts and feelings. There were also difficulties in obtaining reliable data from different observers in different laboratories. So by today's scientific standards the data from introspection experiments were unreliable.

Wundt was aware of the flaws in his introspection research and acknowledged that the process of introspection interrupted the natural thinking process. He spent his career revising his introspection methodology and trying to improve it.

Methodology

The system of methods used in a particular area of study.

The Leipzig laboratory

In 1875 Wilhelm Wundt accepted a position as full professor at the University of Leipzig, which is considered to be the historical home of experimental scientific psychology. He was eventually awarded space for a psychology laboratory. Research began there in 1879, and studies focused on three primary areas: sensation, perception, and psychophysics.

What did Wundt study?

Wundt studied the psychophysics of light and color at his Leipzig laboratory and examined broad questions of sensation and perception, such as how the brain turned electrical activity in the eye into images. He also investigated hearing, including research on frequency (pitch), beat, tone, and tone intervals.

Wundt also investigated the topic of attention, which plays an important role in perception. Attention is an awareness of the here and now; but an individual cannot consciously experience all available events and information at any one time, so attention is selective. Wundt believed that the mind could attend to events that happened both sequentially (one after the other) and simultaneously (at the same time).

Curriculum Context

It may be useful to understand how Wundt was influenced by the experiments of Fechner and Helmholz.

Elementalism

Wundt also developed a theory called elementalism. He thought psychologists should analyze conscious processes and divide them into elements (that is,

Methods of Knowing

People come to "know" something in different ways. With the tenacity method something is considered to be true because it has always been true. With the authority method something becomes true because an authority has told us it is true. With the empiricism method something is true because we have experienced it via our senses. Philosophers use rationalism, which relies on logic and reason to reach a conclusion.

The most reliable and valid way of knowing something is the scientific method, in which scientists use controlled laboratory investigations to establish knowledge.

Science is self-correcting because it allows for verification and change based on the results of experiments conducted in laboratories. When psychology became a science, psychologists also began to use controlled investigations.

smaller parts and processes). According to Wundt, the elements of consciousness were connected, and these connections could be determined by research. Wundt was discussing what we now call neural networks in the brain and how they communicate via neural pathways.

Timing of mental processes

Wundt extended the concept of elementalism to the belief that certain mental processes took a fixed amount of time to complete. He believed that when the same thought was repeated constantly, the connection between its elements became more developed with each use. Wundt found that people got better at a task after practice, but that after a certain point they reached a fixed fastest-response time.

The concept of association

Wundt showed that the mind was designed to perceive the world at different levels of experience. He demonstrated this with a memory task. People were asked to look briefly at a number of random letters of the alphabet and then recall as many letters as possible. Wundt then presented words to his subjects, who recalled a similar number of words as they had previously recalled letters, even though each word had more than one letter. This suggested that when people organized the information (letters) into larger units (words), they were able to deal with more information.

Drawing on data like these, Wundt suggested laws of association. First, there was fusion or blending of feelings. He used the word "feelings" to refer to many things, from emotions to sounds. Second, Wundt believed that two or more feelings could merge to form a single feeling, even though they were independent initially. He also believed that similar things were more likely to be associated.

Brain and nerve cell theories

Wundt's most important book was called the *Principles of Physiological Psychology* (1873–1874). It described his view of how the brain worked. He thought the brain to be a complex organ of fluid chemicals, which were sometimes more active in one region, and sometimes in another. He believed that the entire brain constantly shared in the same chemical-mental activity.

Neuroscience

The study of the structure and function of the brain.

Wundt, therefore, made important contributions to neuroscience. Although his view of the brain was not correct in all the details, it was basically on target, and his work has continued relevance to contemporary neuroscience research.

Curriculum Context

Many curricula expect students to summarize Wundt's contribution to experimental psychology.

Wundt also came up with a theory on the structure of the nervous system, speculating that there had to be a chemical component to the conduction of nerve impulses. He believed that nerve cells sent out three types of chemical processes to other cells. Unipolar (or one-ended) cells could send out only one type, bipolar (or two-ended) cells could send out two types, and multipolar cells could send out multiple chemical processes. According to Wundt, it was the connections that bipolar and multipolar cells made that allowed for behavioral complexity.

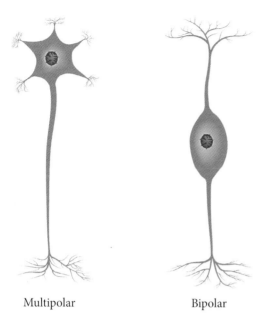

This diagram shows multipolar and bipolar nerve cells. Multiple connections allow for neural control of complex behavior, just as Wundt anticipated.

Multipolar   Bipolar

Structuralism

Edward Bradford Titchener (1867–1927), a student of Wundt's, popularized the scientific study of the psychology of the mind in the United States. The focus of Titchener's work was on mental events—especially the contents of mental events. In Titchener's view the fundamental task for psychological research was to discover the nature of conscious elements. He wanted to analyze thoughts into their component parts so that he could discover the underlying structure of the mind. As a result, he decided to give his theories of psychology the label of structuralism.

In contrast with Titchener's view, Wundt thought that complex mental phenomena could not be studied by introspection. Titchener, however, strongly disagreed, firmly believing that all mental phenomena could be scientifically studied in the laboratory.

Functionalism

The school of functionalist psychology began in the late 19th century, shortly after psychology separated from philosophy as a distinct scientific discipline. Functionalism refers to an approach to studying psychology, rather than a particular theory.

Before functionalism most of psychology was based on observation and description. Functionalists sought to show what purposes mental processes served and how they helped an individual function.

The origins of functionalism

Prior to functionalism the most common method or approach in psychology was structuralism. Structuralism (or structural psychology) was concerned with identifying and describing mental processes (primarily consciousness) using a method known as introspection. Structuralists also wanted to break consciousness down into its individual parts, believing they could only understand how a mental process worked if each part was identified.

An introspectionist had to follow strict procedures. Many researchers found the method too difficult and unpredictable, and the results differed depending on the person. For a method to have scientific validity, it had to give the same result whoever used it.

Another reason why people found structuralism a limited way of studying psychology was related to the old philosophical problem of the mind–body split. Early psychologists believed that the mind and body were separate but working in parallel. Changes in the mind corresponded with changes in the body, but neither could influence the other. This view did not make a great deal of sense to its critics. To them it seemed as though the mind clearly controlled the body, and the body also seemed to influence the mind at times.

Curriculum Context

Students should be aware of the limitations of introspection as a method of analyzing mental processes.

William James

William James (1842–1910) was the creator of functionalism. He based his philosophy on the notion of pragmatism. An idea was only worthwhile if it had some particular purpose. James' interest in the usefulness of mental processes became the basis of the functionalist movement. In the *Principles of Psychology* (1890), James outlined a new kind of psychology that still used introspection as the main method of examining how the mind worked.

James believed the individual had certain needs, and that the environment could provide certain solutions. The role of the mind was to mediate between the two. He thought that his mind worked in the way it did because it helped him adjust to the world around him. This belief that consciousness had a purpose immediately set him apart from structuralism. He also believed that to understand the use and purpose of consciousness, one had to view it as a whole, rather than breaking it down into its parts.

James devoted a great deal of his book to physiology (the physical functions of the human body) and its effect on mental processes, and he categorized certain types of activity as the results of different kinds of

Pragmatism
The use that can be made of knowledge and ideas.

Regular commuters like these in London, England, repeat the same journey day after day. James believed that such habitual actions require only limited input from the mind, freeing it to concentrate on new tasks or thoughts.

Adaptation

The work of Charles Darwin on adaptation and evolution was a major cause of scientific interest in the purpose of natural processes. Darwin proposed that many animals' physical features and behaviors were adaptive. That is, animals behaved in the way they did because it helped them survive and function in their environment.

Over time organisms that had inherited the tendency to engage in adaptive behaviors were the most successful in surviving, reproducing, and passing this tendency on to their offspring. The idea that behavior had a purpose (and that animal behavior was worth studying) became a central belief of the functionalists.

interaction between the mind and body. For example, he thought that habits and instincts were a product of the brain and perceptual system, with only limited input from the mind. Consciousness, reason, and self, on the other hand, he thought to be primarily a result of mental activity. However, James showed that the mental and the physical affected each other.

James believed that experimentation and studies comparing people with animals could also be used in psychology. He also thought that studying animals, children, people of other cultures, and even mentally ill people could help develop psychology as a science.

The reflex arc

In 1896 John Dewey (1859–1952) published a paper entitled "The Reflex Arc Concept in Psychology." The term "reflex arc" was used to describe an organism's response to the world. Dewey used the example of a child viewing a flame, touching it, and burning her fingers. The child would reflexively withdraw her fingers, but thereafter would not touch flame, remembering how she had been burned in the past. The sequence of events had changed the child's perception of the flame from being attractive to being dangerous. Viewed in this way, the reflex arc serves a particular purpose: to help us avoid danger and injury.

Reflexively
Without conscious thought.

James Rowland Angell

James Rowland Angell (1869–1949) studied under Dewey and James. His most famous work was *Psychology: An Introductory Study of the Structure and Function of Human Consciousness.* Angell concentrated on functional explanations of various phenomena, always trying to show how they helped a person adapt to the environment. He also insisted on a close and interactive relationship between the mental and the physical and was concerned with the way in which mental processes developed.

Harvey A. Carr

Under Harvey A. Carr (1873–1954) functionalism reached its peak of popularity. Carr realized that psychology could only develop as a science if its methods were considered to be properly scientific. As a result, functionalism relied more and more on experimentation to collect data. Experimentation was more objective than introspection: in carefully controlled experiments it was more likely that different researchers would find the same results, making the experiments more scientifically valid.

In *Psychology: A Study of Mental Activity* (1925) Carr surveyed the field of psychology, focusing mainly on the ways in which behavior could be viewed as helping a person adapt to the environment. Each kind of mental activity, such as thinking, remembering, perceiving, and reasoning, was said to have a purpose, guiding a person's behavior.

The legacy of functionalism

Because functionalism was more a method of psychology than a theory, over time it was absorbed into other systems. Its most obvious influence was ultimately in testing mental abilities, because psychologists thought they played an important role in people's capacity to succeed in school and at work.

Curriculum Context

Students should be able to describe the influence of functionalism on contemporary theories of psychology.

Gestalt Psychology

Gestalt psychology was a reaction against earlier psychological approaches that had attempted to separate the functions of the mind. The German word *gestalt* means "form" or "whole," and Gestalt psychologists saw the mind as a whole.

Gestalt psychology began in Germany in 1910. While traveling by train, Czech-born psychologist Max Wertheimer (1880–1943) saw flashing lights at a railroad crossing that resembled lights encircling a theater marquee and was seized by an idea. He got off the train in Frankfurt and bought a motion picture toy called a zoetrope. In his hotel room he made his own picture strips, consisting not of identifiable objects but abstract lines, ranging from vertical to horizontal. By varying these elements, he was able to investigate the conditions that contribute to the illusion of motion pictures, in which stationary objects shown in rapid succession appear to move because the brain cannot perceive them as individual elements so sees them as one moving image. This effect is known as "apparent movement." Wertheimer called it the phi phenomenon.

According to Wertheimer, the phi phenomenon disproved previous theories of how individual stimuli were perceived. He proposed that the brain perceived any stimulus as a meaningful "whole," rather than an assembly of separate data.

Founders of Gestalt theory

Wertheimer studied the phi phenomenon with his two assistants, Wolfgang Köhler (1887–1967) and Kurt Koffka (1886–1941). They published their findings in 1912 in a paper entitled "Experimental Studies of the Perception of Movement." Convinced that the segmented approach to the study of human behavior taken by structuralists and other psychologists was inadequate, these three became the central figures of

Phi phenomenon
An illusion in which an appearance of movement is created by a series of still images.

the German Gestalt school. Wertheimer criticized traditional forms of logic for ignoring the way in which people group and reorganize the things they perceive when solving problems.

Logic
Reasoning conducted according to strict rules of validity.

The least effort

According to perception theory at that time, our senses picked up information about the physical world as simple, often unnoticeable sensations. For example, background conversation was thought to be heard (sensed) but not perceived (listened to) because it was experienced outside of a person's attention. Earlier psychologists, particularly those of the structuralist school, had split up these phenomena into their individual components, such as feelings, images, and sensations. This view did not allow for the additional meaning given to phenomena when we perceive them as a whole.

Similarity (left)
We perceive these 20 separate dots as two columns of orange dots and two columns of yellow dots.

Proximity (right)
We perceive this figure as three groups of two lines or three stripes rather than as six separate lines.

In 1923 Max Wertheimer published a paper entitled "Theory of Form," which was nicknamed "the dot essay" because it was illustrated with abstract patterns of dots and lines. Wertheimer claimed that our inborn tendency to perceive elements as "belonging together" enhances certain forms. This enhancement occurs with elements that look alike (similarity grouping), are situated close together (proximity grouping), or have visual continuity (closure). This enhancement is shown in the two examples here of proximity and similarity.

Wertheimer claimed that an observer's nervous system organizes the stimulus experienced into a whole, or Gestalt, rather than making the effort to perceive many individual impressions. The brain looks for a shortcut, organizing stimuli into packages of information, just as we might put all our papers concerning one subject into a file or all the photos from one vacation in one album. Wertheimer, and later Köhler, believed that the brain's organization of perceived things into "wholes" was reflected in the makeup of the nervous system.

Modern neuropsychology has challenged most of the Gestalt ideas about how the brain is organized. Although we now know that nerve fibers are arranged into patterns that restrict their function, there is no evidence for the existence of the whole figure models that Wertheimer and his colleagues believed in.

Wertheimer's concept of organization was called *Prägnanz* ("conciseness"). It stated that when things are considered as wholes, the amount of energy exerted in thinking is minimized. His theory can be extended to thinking about people. For example, it is easier to think of a group of football players as a team rather than as individual players. This concept is seen most clearly if one tries to think about more than one sports team at a time: It is far easier for the mind to consider the players as two or three wholes (teams) than as many individual members.

Gestalt and social psychology

Another central idea of Gestalt theory was that of the figure against a background. For example, in a painting Gestalt theory maintains that the entire picture is important—the landscape and the figures—not simply one element, such as the human figure. Gestalt psychologists see the individual as a figure against a background of social relationships with

Curriculum Context

Students may be asked to outline the basic principles of Gestalt theory, such as figure-ground.

Gestalt and the Bauhaus

Many of the ideas of the Gestalt psychologists inspired the artists and designers of the Bauhaus: a major German school of art and design in the late 1920s and early 1930s that influenced design and architecture worldwide.

The Gestalt psychologist Karlfried von Dürckheim (1896–1988) lectured at the Bauhaus between 1930 and 1931 to an audience that included artists Paul Klee (1879–1940), Wassily Kandinsky (1866–1944), and Josef Albers (1888–1976). Klee had known about Max Wertheimer's research as early as 1925 and used some of the diagrams from Wertheimer's 1923 "dot essay" in his 1930s paintings. Albers reawoke interest in the idea of "simultaneous contrast": the phenomenon, known for centuries by artists, in which the same color seems to have a different brightness or intensity depending on its contrast with a background color. For example, a particular hue of red shown against a green background (high contrast) seems much brighter than the same hue shown against an orange background. This phenomenon supported the Gestalt idea that we perceive wholes rather than isolated parts— seeing only dynamic relationships between figures and their backgrounds rather than the figures alone.

Many artists embraced Gestalt theory because it seemed to provide scientific validation of age-old principles of composition and page layout. Gestalt theory became associated with the modernist belief that all art is essentially abstract design, and that design is at heart an abstract, formal activity. Meaning, or the subject being represented in an art form, became less important than the form or organization of the elements.

others. A person is not only part of her own life, she is also among other people. When a group of people work together, they are rarely a collection of independent personalities. Instead, the common enterprise becomes their shared concern, and each person works as a functioning part of the whole group.

Wertheimer's perception of how we relate to groups anticipates some of the findings of cross-cultural psychology, which contrasts traditional Western views of the individual's psychology with those of other cultures in which the psychology of the whole group is taken into consideration. Such cultures take a much more holistic view of individuals compared with traditional psychology.

Holistic

Characterized by the belief that the parts of something are interconnected and can only be explained by reference to the whole.

Gestalt in the United States

Wertheimer, Koffka, and Köhler extended the Gestalt approach to other areas of perception, problem solving, learning, and thinking. Koffka performed original studies on perception and investigated how patterns of behavior develop in the early years. Köhler carried out important studies on chimpanzees, investigating how they learn and think, make tools, and, he claimed, show insight in planned actions. Due to his efforts Gestalt ideas were widely accepted into other schools of psychology.

Gestalt therapy

Gestalt therapy draws on the central ideas of Gestalt theory, such as the need for closure. It is a form of humanistic therapy and attempts to apply the laws of perception to a person's life experience. Humanistic therapy suggests that each individual must be understood within the context of his or her own life. Gestalt therapy emphasizes a whole, or holistic, view of the individual, focusing on the entire person and the client's sense of self-awareness. Just as a "gestalt" is a figure or pattern that can be distinguished against a field of perception or background, so Gestalt therapy encourages individuals to look at themselves (the figure) against the background of their own lives and experiences, considering the whole picture rather than simply thinking about their internal feelings. It is important in Gestalt therapy for individuals to recognize who they are at the moment. Patients are often asked to recount unresolved or traumatic experiences and to say how they feel after recounting them. By acknowledging their feelings, they gain a better idea of the effect that experience has had on them and learn how to cope.

Fritz Perls (1893–1970) and his wife Laura (1905–1990) developed Gestalt therapy in the 1950s. Perls saw the task of psychotherapy as one of emphasizing the difference between figure (the patient) and ground

Curriculum Context

It can be very useful to examine how psychological theories influence different forms of therapy.

Traumatic
Emotionally disturbing or distressing.

(experience) in the areas, or gestalten (the plural of gestalt), that reflected the patient's needs.

According to Perls, a healthy person organizes experiences into well-differentiated gestalten so there is clear understanding of, and distinction between, a feeling and its context. The individual can then decide on an appropriate response. For example, someone whose body is dehydrated will become aware of the gestalt of thirst and will get a drink. An angry person who is aware of his or her feeling similarly has a choice of responses: either to express the anger, to make others aware of it, or to release it in some other way. A person who is unaware may suppress the feeling and so suffer frustration. On the other hand, a neurotic person continually interferes with the formation of gestalten, refusing to acknowledge how he feels at a particular time. He is unable to deal effectively with certain needs because he interrupts and avoids the formation of a relevant gestalt.

Gestalt therapy may be based on one-to-one discussion, as shown here, but can also involve group work in which individuals are encouraged to express to each other how they feel.

The legacy of gestalt

Today Gestalt theory's influence in the field of psychology is not that noticeable because many of its findings have been absorbed by more recent viewpoints, but in the history of psychology the Gestalt movement was an important corrective to earlier approaches. Gestalt theories have also had a profound effect on holistic ideas of therapy.

Psychoanalysis

Sigmund Freud developed psychoanalysis more than 100 years ago, and it has had an enduring effect on psychology and on Western culture. Some of the early ideas of psychoanalysis are not as popular or accepted as in the past, and few psychoanalysts still believe everything that Freud said was correct.

When we use the term psychoanalysis, we are really talking about two things. First, psychoanalysis has to do with a particular theory of human behavior. Its theories state that all human behavior is motivated (caused by something), but that motivations are often hidden from the individual (unconscious).

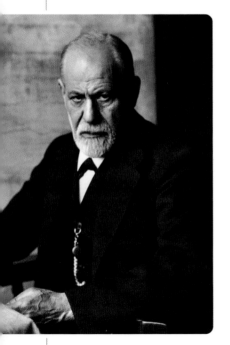

Sigmund Freud, the Viennese doctor who founded psychoanalysis, had a profound influence on the intellectual history of the 20th century.

Second, psychoanalysis refers to a kind of therapy or counseling for people who are distressed or troubled. Psychoanalytic therapy is derived from psychoanalytic theories of behavior, and the therapist or counselor seeks to understand what kinds of unconscious forces might be making the person distressed or unhappy.

Major points of theory

The most important figure in early psychoanalysis was its originator, Sigmund Freud (1856–1939). Freud was a physician who frequently treated patients with inexplicable disorders that seemed not to have been caused by any underlying illness or injury. Freud became convinced that their suffering was real and was probably caused by some hidden psychological problem. He began to question his patients about emotional and personal experiences, trying to determine the cause of their problems. Using this approach, he developed his technique of psychoanalysis and formulated ideas about human behavior, later known as psychoanalytic theory. Psychoanalytic theory is a complex system for understanding human behavior, but is more easily understood by concentrating on three main principles.

The first of these principles is that unconscious forces motivate most human behavior. This means that people are generally unaware of the reasons why they act the way they do.

The second principle is that past experience shapes the way a person behaves in the present. What happened in the past is extremely important in determining how a person will react to events in the present and future.

The third principle is that psychoanalysis enables people to cope with distress and trouble by helping them understand the unconscious forces that motivate them and the influences of their earlier experiences.

Tenets of Freudian theory

An underlying principle of Freud's theory was that the main motivating force behind human behavior is an unconscious drive for sexuality. He suggested that all human beings, even children, have strong sexual impulses, and that these impulses motivate all behavior. This is a major source of difficulty for the individual because sexual behavior is not socially acceptable. The combination of this motivating force and the realities of social life results in conflict. The outcome of this conflict determines people's behavior and personalities in later life.

The sexual aspect of Freud's theory was particlarly shocking at the time in which he lived because sex and sexuality were topics that were not to be discussed. It is still criticized today, mainly due to Freud's insistence that children have unconscious sexual motivations.

The second major principle of Freudian theory is that mental life is dynamic, driven by energy between the

Curriculum Context

Students need to understand the basic principles of Freudian psychoanalysis.

body and mind. Freud believed that the personality or psyche resides in three distinct levels of consciousness. Part of the personality is conscious and is concerned with thoughts and feelings. A second part of personality is the preconscious, consisting mainly of memories and thoughts that, while not conscious at the moment, can become conscious. The third—and to Freud the most important—part of the personality is the unconscious, in which lie wishes, desires, and motivations of which people cannot become aware.

Id, ego, and superego

Freud also believed that the personality consists of different structures that manage the motivational force. He gave them Latin names: the id ("it"), the ego ("I"), and the superego ("over I"). The source of motivation is in the id, which is in the unconscious. In the id are impulses, motivations, and desires.

Freud stated that the id's main task is to satisfy impulses and desires by discharging the energy behind them, resulting in pleasure. The ego tries to plan ways in which the id can release its energy and satisfy its impulses, and as such is mainly conscious. The ego is rational and operates according to what Freud termed the "reality principle," which states that

Preconscious

The part of the mind below the level of consciousness, from which memories and emotions can be recalled.

Curriculum Context

Freud's theory of the personality underlay much 20th-century thought and art.

Accessing the Unconscious

Sigmund Freud used various techniques to gain access to unconscious material. One was free association, in which the patient was encouraged to say whatever came to mind freely and without censorship. Freud then searched for themes and clues to the patient's disorder.

Another therapeutic technique was dream analysis. Freud asked patients to write down and describe their dreams in detail, believing that in dreams the person's unconscious wishes and desires were revealed. In most cases these wishes and desires were not revealed directly, but were suggested through metaphors and imagery; what the dream appeared to say was not necessarily its literal meaning. The importance of dreams was to indicate the nature of the unconscious.

desires and impulses can be fulfilled, but only in certain ways. The ego is what keeps the individual from doing whatever he or she (or rather the id) pleases at any given time. The superego operates to constrain the ego from allowing the id to satisfy impulses. It is both conscious and unconscious, and can be compared to a person's conscience. The superego ensures that the person's behavior conforms to society's expectations.

Freud theorized that human personality develops from these unconscious conflicts and their outcomes. From the moment of birth the id's desire for pleasure is curbed by rules imposed by parents and society. Children's sense of bodily pleasure shifts as they grow from infancy to adulthood through five stages of psychosexual development. Each stage involves a conflict between the desire for pleasure and the need to live by the rules of the real world.

The oral and anal stages

According to Freud, during the first or oral stage (infancy) the person's focus for pleasure (sexuality) is through the mouth and the act of sucking and taking in nourishment. The conflict at this stage arises from the process of weaning. Failure to resolve the conflict at this stage can result either in a great dependency on others or in an aggressive and sarcastic personality.

In the second or anal stage (just past infancy) the passing of feces becomes the focus of pleasure. The conflict at this stage arises from being toilet

Weaning
Moving a baby from breast-feeding or bottle to solid food.

Is this child teething? According to Freudian theory, young children put objects in their mouths in an attempt to rediscover the oral gratification they received as infants while feeding at their mothers' breasts.

trained and the way in which children learn to control their bowel movements. Failure to resolve this conflict can result in excessively fussy (anal retentive) or slovenly (anal expulsive) behavior in later life.

The phallic stage

During the third, phallic stage (early childhood) the phallus is the object that provides pleasure, so the genital area becomes the focus of attention. This is accompanied by feelings of attraction to the opposite sex. Freud suggested that the natural object for a young child's affection is the opposite-sex parent. A successful resolution of this conflict ends in the child identifying with the same-sex parent and no longer wishing to possess the opposite-sex parent. Failure to resolve this conflict results in later sexual problems.

Latency and genital stages

Between the ages of about 6 and 12, said Freud, unconscious conflicts subside as children make conscious social adjustments. This is called the latency period because unconscious developmental conflicts are latent or hidden. The final, genital, stage occurs during adolescence, when children begin to have sexual feelings toward others closer to their own age. During this stage children struggle toward "sensible love," and conflict arises as they move away from the parents toward friendships with others. Freud believed that successful resolution of this conflict was important to develop healthy adult relationships.

Curriculum Context

Many curricula ask students to describe Freud's theories about human personality development.

Defense mechanisms

Defense mechanisms formed another important part of Freud's theories. The defense mechanisms develop as a means for the ego to protect itself from the id and also from the superego. Some of these mechanisms prevent the id impulses from being fulfilled; others are designed to fulfill them in relatively harmless ways.

Carl Gustav Jung

Carl Gustav Jung (1875–1961) had a great interest in mental disorders. Jung's theories developed over a period of years and ultimately differed dramatically from Freud's.

One of the main features of Jung's theory was the collective unconscious. Jung believed that individuals had two kinds of unconscious mind, a personal one that contained their own memories and a collective one that contained material that was common to all people. Material in the collective unconscious was organized around ideas that were common to people throughout history and across cultures. Jung called these ideas archetypes. Ideas about god and the self were also special, more powerful archetypes. He drew on anthropology, literature (especially myths, legends, and fairy tales), alchemy, and theology to develop these theories.

The primary defense mechanism described by Freud is repression: an energy force that serves to keep the impulses in the id from escaping. Repression requires effort and energy, however, and does not always work. It is not in operation, for example, when a person is sleeping. Freud believed therefore that dreams contain material derived from the unconscious.

Other defense mechanisms include projection: the tendency to observe traits or patterns of behavior in others that correspond to people's own unconscious impulses. Displacement allows people to fulfill their id impulses but changes the object. Reaction formation is a defense mechanism that takes an unacceptable impulse and turns it into its extreme opposite, while sublimation turns an unacceptable impulse into another, socially acceptable one.

Psychoanalysis as treatment

Freud believed that patients displayed hysteria because they were unable to properly resolve conflicts at some stage of their development. To treat these patients, Freud needed to be able to see what resided in their unconscious. He believed that therapists had to get to know patients really well to understand the events that

Hysteria
Exaggerated or uncontrollable emotion.

Alfred Adler

Alfred Adler (1870–1937) was a physician who initially worked closely with Freud but developed his own views that were quite different from Freud's. Adler believed that all behavior is motivated by people trying to get or achieve something specific, rather than by some internal force. Adler believed that these goals and strivings are the main determinant of personality.

All individuals strive to achieve as much as they can in life, and they will often try to do better than other people. Under the surface most individuals feel as though they are worth little, and so they strive for superiority to compensate for their feelings of incompetence and inferiority.

Adler also believed different styles of parenting, including both pampering and rejection, could have negative influences on children's development. He also thought that birth order was an important determinant of personality. Being an only child, first-born, last-born, or a middle child could all affect a person's later life roles, relationships, and behaviors.

might have shaped their experiences. Consequently therapists and patients talk at length about the patients' past histories, experiences, and memories.

Ego psychology

Freud's daughter Anna (1895–1982) was particularly interested in the role of the ego. This focus on the ego began a movement called ego psychology, which was taken up by Heinz Hartmann (1894–1970) and Ernst Kris (1900–1957). They argued that the ego was more important than the id and the superego. They thought that the ego contained a "conflict-free sphere," and that it was not just an arbiter between the id and the superego, but used strategy to control them.

Arbiter
Something that settles a dispute or has ultimate authority in a matter.

According to the ego psychologists, patients experience mental problems because they have a weak ego, or because their ego is unable to deal with the id and the superego. Psychoanalysts can help patients solve their problems by making their egos more powerful and by making sure that they can adapt themselves to their environment. Psychoanalytic therapists achieve this by offering themselves as an example of someone with a strong, well-adapted ego. Ego psychologists believe that psychoanalysts can offer their own strong personalities as a substitute for the weak personalities of their patients.

Many psychoanalysts criticized ego psychology because they felt a patient could become entirely dominated by the psychoanalyst's personality. During the early 1950s Jacques Lacan (1901–1981) argued that ego psychologists had forgotten that psychoanalysis was about analyzing and not about educating.

Lacan argued that children develop their identity (their ego, or sense of self) when they are capable of recognizing that the image they see in a mirror is their own reflection. This happens some time between the age of 6 and 18 months. It is not a natural ability; an adult has to explain it to them. Thus, in Lacan's theory language is essential for the development of identity.

Self-psychology

The tradition of self-psychology within contemporary psychoanalysis originated in the work of Heinz Kohut (1913–1981). Kohut did not agree with the ideas of the ego psychologists. He was convinced that ego psychology was too rigid and did not see psychoanalysis as a technique for improving people's adjustment to the environment. Kohut tried to develop a theory that was based more on human relationships. He talked about the "selfobject," that is to say, an object as experienced by and within the self. For example, it is more important to know how people think about their parents than who those parents really are.

Pathology

Physical or mental disease.

Narcissistic

Having excessive interest in oneself and one's appearance.

Curriculum Context

An awareness of the new approaches to psychology is required by some curricula.

Kohut described the normal stages of development, and various forms of pathology, with reference to this selfobject. He argued that normal children develop a nuclear, or core, self as a result of good, responsive relationships with their environment. This nuclear self comprises two aspects: a grandiose, narcissistic self that makes children feel they are perfect and brilliant, and an idealized image of the parents that makes children feel that others are perfect and brilliant. Kohut believed that mental problems could be explained in terms of conflicts within the self. He did not agree with the traditional image of the psychoanalyst as a distant figure. Rather, the analyst had to be warm, sensitive, and empathic (identify with the patient).

Relational psychoanalysis

Among the most recent developments in psychoanalysis was the work of Stephen A. Mitchell (1946–2000). Mitchell started from the observation that there are many different theories in contemporary psychoanalysis. He then argued that these theories could be classified under one of two headings: They are either in favor of Freud's model of the drive (instinct) or they are in favor of a model that emphasizes relationships between subjects.

Mitchell's work is often described as the integrated relational model. He said that Freud's model of the drive does not take into account the fact that people are involved in relationships with other people.

One of the most important notions in Mitchell's theory was the relational matrix—a typically human pattern of interaction comprising the self, the object, and the possible ties between the self and the object. Mitchell used the notion of the relational matrix to interpret many traditional psychoanalytic topics in a new way.

Psychoanalysis today

Psychoanalytic theory is controversial, and the main focus of this controversy concerns the notion of childhood sexuality and the events that occur during the development of the personality. Most of Freud's writings were concerned with the experience of young men, and much of his theorizing about young women was either incomplete or frustratingly vague.

A further criticism of psychoanalysis is that it is not rigorously scientifically based. Freud did not follow traditional scientific methods. He did not generate hypotheses and test them independently. Neither did he test people on any standardized instrument or scale.

Hypotheses

(singular: hypothesis) Proposed explanations based on limited evidence and used as the starting points for further investigation.

The Methodology of Child Psychoanalysis

Melanie Klein was one of the first psychoanalysts to apply Freud's ideas to children. She was convinced that a child psychoanalyst should only concentrate on the nature and development of the child's unconscious fantasies. She devoted most of her time to the treatment of children suffering from severe mental problems. She put great emphasis on the fantasy world of young children and did not hesitate to ask them daring questions, for example, their thoughts about death and sexuality. She believed young children often experience feelings of extreme anger and anxiety. Fantasies are a way of coming to terms with these feelings. Klein used play techniques in her work with children, believing that it revealed their psychological impulses.

Little Red Riding Hood meets the wolf. Klein believed that, like fairy tales, fantasies provide a way for children to come to terms with anxiety or extreme anger.

Phenomenology and Humanism

Phenomenology was a philosophical perspective that emphasized the importance of an individual's subjective experience of reality. Later this idea was incorporated in humanistic psychology, which emphasized people's potential for personal growth and stressed the influence of conscious experience on human behavior.

Edmund Husserl (1859–1938) first described the approach he termed phenomenology in 1913: The term came from the Greek words *phenomenon*, meaning appearance, and *logos*, meaning study. Husserl said it was important to study how people perceived and experienced events, placing emphasis on each individual's interpretation of a situation. French philosopher Maurice Merleau-Ponty (1908–1961) went on to develop his own phenomenological theory. He stated that perception was not a general process but one unique to each perceiver.

Phenomenologists believe conscious life experiences, whether positive or negative, cause people to form models, or images of themselves. Behavior adds to and potentially reinforces these models (self-concepts).

Humanism
In the 1940s the work of Charlotte Bühler (1893–1974) became influential. Bühler identified four basic tendencies: to strive for personal satisfaction in sex and love; to adapt and limit oneself for the purpose of fitting in, belonging, and gaining security; to strive for self-expression and creative accomplishments; to work toward upholding order and integrating with society.

The term humanism usually refers to a philosophy that is optimistic about human possibilities. Humanistic psychologists took this approach to understanding behavior, incorporating the philosophy of phenomenology and opposing reductionism. Gestalt

Reductionism

The practice of breaking behavior down into parts and assuming it is the result of conditioning or physiological drives.

psychologists had already studied people's perceptions, suggesting that people never sensed the environment as it was but only as it made "sense" to the brain. Humanistic psychologists suggested that it was people's interpretations of perceived situations that influenced their actions. Thus to truly understand human behavior, researchers needed to consider entire people, their social networks, and the emotional and spiritual meanings they sought in their lives.

Abraham Maslow

Psychologist Abraham Maslow (1908–1970) believed that human motivation results from a series of key drives and insisted that the individual is conscious of these drives. He suggested that people have a core set of needs that motivate and influence their behavior and that they have a need to reach their full potential.

Curriculum Context

Students may be asked to predict behavior about meeting needs based on Maslow's theory.

Maslow's Hierarchy of Needs

Maslow's hierarchy of needs is usually represented as a pyramid. The base of the pyramid shows the physical necessities of life; the top depicts self-actualization, or the achievement of complete psychological health or potential. Maslow emphasized that lower needs on the hierarchy must be met and maintained before the higher needs can be achieved.

Generally, the lower needs, such as hunger, must be at least partly satisfied before an individual will feel strongly motivated by needs higher up the hierarchy. There are some exceptions, however. For example, in the past some artists have chosen to starve rather than give up their art.

7 SELF-ACTUALIZATION NEEDS: to find self-fulfillment and realize one's potential

6 AESTHETIC NEEDS: symmetry, order, and beauty

5 COGNITVE NEEDS: to know, understand, and explore

4. ESTEEM NEEDS: to achieve, be competent, and gain approval and recognition

3. BELONGINGNESS AND LOVE NEEDS: to affiliate with others, be accepted, and belong

2. SAFETY NEEDS: to feel secure and safe, out of danger

1. PHYSIOLOGICAL NEEDS: hunger, thirst, and so forth

Carl Rogers

Psychotherapist Carl Rogers (1902–1987) is often associated with the notion of self-psychology, which states that a person's concept of him- or herself helps determine his or her perception of experiences. Rogers was influential in developing person- or client-centered therapy, which promoted personal growth and the attainment of self-actualization.

Curriculum Context

Students should be aware of the importance of Carl Rogers' ideas in the development of humanistic psychology and therapy.

Self-concept

Rogers's style of therapy developed from his theories about the development of personality and the self-concept, and from his many clinical interactions with clients during therapy sessions. His experience working with these clients enabled him to construct his theories about human potential, in which he placed importance on the individual's personal experience and proposed that personality could be considered as one central idea of "self." Rogers viewed the self-concept as a conscious experience. He proposed that people are aware of their view of self, behaving in ways that are in line with this concept.

Rogers suggested that as people experience life, their perceptions of reality either confirm or contradict their self-concept. Rogers proposed that the development of self begins from children's interactions with their parents and immediate social group. The development of a healthy self-concept is the result of a stable and nurturing environment that recognizes children's need for acceptance and love.

Rogers also said that human needs can be met either conditionally or unconditionally. Conditional love refers to an environment where children are only given the love and acceptance they desire if they meet expectations. Unconditional love and acceptance refer to an environment that nurtures children's development regardless of attainment.

This child is being scolded by her father. According to Rogers, children who still feel loved despite naughty behavior will be happier and more secure than children who feel that love is conditional on their good behavior.

Congruence and incongruence

According to Rogers, a self-concept that is supported by reality is congruent, meaning that both the individual's inner perceptions and outer experiences are consistent. He also proposed that an environment in which the individual experiences unconditional, positive regard assists in the promotion of self-worth.

As a person's self-concept develops and remains congruent, a self-fulfilling prophecy can develop. This means that individuals begin to behave in ways that match their perceived sense of self. For example, if a woman views herself as responsible and sensible, she will act in ways that confirm these beliefs. And if she encounters or experiences information that contrasts with her self-concept, she will dismiss or avoid it.

On the other hand, if an individual's self-concept differs from reality, this creates incongruence. For example, if a boy works hard in school but is criticized unfairly by his parents as "lazy," his two experiences are incongruent, and he may develop a self-concept of unworthiness that does not match reality. The wider the gap between

Client-centered Psychotherapy

Carl Rogers believed that the role of the therapist was to provide an environment that fostered self-development, helping clients discover solutions to their own problems. He emphasized that the relationship between the client and the therapist had to be based on honesty. Therapists had to be open to their clients' reactions and experiences in therapy sessions. This helped create an environment that was safe and comfortable for the clients, enabling them to express themselves freely to another, nonjudgmental person.

Rogers also proposed that unconditional positive regard ensured that people developed to their highest potential. This regard needed to come from individuals themselves (congruence) and from their worlds (acceptance and love from parents without conditions). Even if a person grew up in a conditional environment and developed inner conflict and incongruence, Rogers maintained that positive change was still possible by fostering an environment of unconditional positive regard in therapy sessions, enabling the individual to develop self-worth and congruence.

Empathy refers to an understanding of another person's emotional experiences or feelings. According to Rogers, to reflect or feed back on a client's experiences, therapists had to provide an accurate level of empathy.

the self and reality, the greater the possibility of confusion or problematic behaviors.

According to Rogers, people function more effectively if they are brought up with unconditional love. If parents only offer conditional love, children may grow up to believe that they need to be perfect to gain acceptance and love from others. This might lead them to set unrealistic expectations for work, social, or personal pursuits. They may never feel truly satisfied with their performance and may be highly critical of their abilities.

Humanistic therapy

Psychologists who adopt a humanistic approach emphasize that people are capable of striving to achieve their full potential. Therapy consists of individual sessions that focus on clients' potential for personal growth. First the therapist stresses the importance of each person learning to accept responsibility for his experiences and interactions. The therapeutic relationship is then used to generate a nurturing environment in which the individual can grow and develop healthy self-concepts.

Rogers suggested that people have aims to develop and enhance themselves, and that this enables them to consciously accept or reject social norms. He used the term self-actualizing in reference to this motivation to achieve independence.

Humanism and psychoanalysis

Psychoanalysis proposes that human behavior can be explained in terms of unconscious desires or processes. Humanism proposes that both the conscious and unconscious need to be considered when trying to understand human motivation and behavior.

Another difference lies in basic perceptions of people. Humanists believe that people have the potential to enhance themselves and take an optimistic view of human nature and behavior. Psychoanalysts view people as primarily engaged in a continual struggle between unconscious conflicts and desires.

Limitations

Humanism's main limitations are considered to be its poor testability, its unrealistic view of human nature, and the inadequate evidence available to support its claims. Humanistic approaches are often considered to have poor testability because the concepts they describe are not easily defined or measured.

Humanistic psychology has also been criticized because its effectiveness as a method of psychotherapy has not been established through research. Instead, therapists have noted its effectiveness by clinical observations of the positive changes in clients' behavior and experience brought about by using this approach.

Nurturing
Caring; encouraging growth or development.

Curriculum Context
Students can usefully compare humanism to other 20th-century schools of psychology.

Behaviorism

Behaviorism arose partly as a backlash against introspection, insisting on measuring only things that could be directly observed in the physical world, a fundamental requirement of sciences such as chemistry and physics.

Before behaviorism psychologists had talked about both people's behavior and the contents of their minds. The behaviorists, however, argued that the mind could not be studied scientifically. They argued that psychology should only concern itself with the way in which events in the world caused changes in animal (including human) behavior.

In the sciences, however, experiments must be repeatable. If a scientist describes the procedure for an experiment, another scientist must be able to perform it and obtain the same results. The behaviorists believed that for psychology to be a true science, it could not depend on any one person's subjective impressions; discussion of mind was meaningless because mental processes cannot be reliably observed.

Ivan Pavlov

Behaviorism had its roots in several developments around the beginning of the 20th century. Among the most important of them were the conditioning experiments conducted by Ivan Pavlov (1849–1936). Pavlov studied the digestive process in dogs and was particularly interested in the production of saliva, which is an involuntary reflex action. Pavlov soon noticed that his dogs began to salivate even before they were given food. The sight of the lab attendants who brought food to the dogs was enough to trigger this response. To test this reaction formally, he rang a bell just before the food was presented. After a while he found that he could make the dogs salivate merely by ringing the bell without giving them any food. He

Subjective
Influenced by personal feelings or opinions.

Saliva
A watery liquid secreted into the mouth that aids chewing, swallowing, and digestion.

also found that additional repetitions of the bell–food connection strengthened the effect, while many repetitions of the bell without food made the effect diminish and eventually go away.

E. L. Thorndike

E. L. Thorndike (1874–1949) was interested in finding out whether dogs and cats could learn by observation. He placed the animals in cages called puzzle boxes that they could open from inside by pressing a lever. He found that when an animal simply observed another animal, or a person, pressing the lever to open the cage, no learning took place. Even when he guided the animal's paw onto the lever, the animal did not learn. But sooner or later the animal would step on the lever by accident, and after this happened many times, the animal eventually learned that stepping on the lever opened the cage and would do so immediately after it was put inside.

It has long been known that dogs salivate at the sight and smell of food; Ivan Pavlov showed that they could also be taught to salivate in response to other stimuli associated with a meal.

Thorndike deduced that a behavior that produces a positive result is likely to be repeated. This behavior seemed to be independent of conscious thought.

The rise of behaviorism

Darwin's theory of natural selection and an acceptance of the idea that people had evolved from lower animals led to a belief in a continuity between people and animals. If there was indeed continuity between people and animals, then "mind" might also have to be taken into account in any attempt to explain animal behavior.

Natural selection

The process by which organisms that are better suited to their environment are more likely to survive and produce more offspring.

Early in the 20th century John B. Watson studied learning in rats. The ideas of Darwinism, coupled with the introspective approach to the study of the mind, demanded that he explain his results in terms of conscious thought by the animals, which he found unacceptable. Watson concluded that for psychology to be a true science, it must study only an organism's observable behavior. We can, he said, observe only a stimulus (an event that takes place before an organism does something) and the response (the behavior that follows). The stimulus could be a signal or some internal event. The response would have to be an observable action.

Watson's principles

Watson proposed some basic principles of behavioristic psychology. The first principle was that psychologists could measure only what happens outside the organism. Introspection and any concept of "mind" were irrelevant. Second, the purpose of psychological research is the prediction and control of behavior. Third, there is no difference between people and animals, except a difference in degree (for example, level of intelligence). Fourth, the behavior of people results entirely from physiological reactions and is not attributable to any nonphysical force.

The conditioned reflex

Watson went on to attempt to explain complex human behavior entirely in terms of the conditioned reflex. He began by rejecting the idea that many common human activities are guided by "instinct." An instinct is a behavior that is hard-wired into the organism and present from birth. Higher animals seem to operate on a mix of hard-wired and learned behaviors.

After observing human infants Watson decided that only a few basic behaviors, such as grasping, sucking,

Curriculum Context

Many curricula ask students to describe the basic principles of behaviorist psychology.

Albert and the Rat

John B. Watson determined that children are born with only a few basic fears: of falling, loud sounds, pain, and of having their bodies restrained. All other fears, he said, were the result of conditioning, as objects or events in their lives became associated with the basic fears.

He first tested this idea on an 11-month-old boy known as Albert. Albert was first introduced to a white laboratory rat. He touched it, stroked it, and played with it completely without fear. Then, just as Albert reached for the rat, experimenters behind the boy struck an iron bar with a hammer. The noise frightened Albert, and after just a few repeats of the experience the rat brought out the same fear response as the loud noise. Now presenting the rat alone would cause Albert to shy away and cry.

Watson conducted subsequent experiments in fear reduction on other children. He found that positive stimuli, such as food, could be used to condition children out of their fears. A child who was afraid of rats was given food while a rat in a cage was placed a long distance away. Each day the cage was moved closer at feeding time, until the child was eating with one hand and stroking the rat with the other.

Behaviorists believe that the common human fear of rats is learned rather than natural.

and random movements of the limbs, were built into every infant. More complex behaviors such as smiling grew out of conditioning, Watson claimed.

Emotions, Watson said, also resulted from conditioning early in life. During experiments he found that newborn babies showed only a few emotional responses: They would exhibit fear when they heard a loud sound, felt pain, or experienced a loss of support; rage when their limbs were restrained; and pleasure when they were stroked or fed. All these responses, he thought, would have evolved as survival mechanisms. As life went on, other stimuli became associated with these experiences. For example, the mother's stroking and feeding would condition the child to "love" its female parent.

Survival mechanisms
Processes that allow an organism to live through difficult circumstances.

Watson believed no one was "instinctively" afraid of, for example, spiders. Such fears were conditioned early on by association with the simple inbuilt fears.

Larynx

The hollow organ holding the vocal cords; the voice box.

Skills and conditioning

According to Watson, even the simplest physical skills are the result of early conditioning. A newborn is constantly bombarded by stimuli, both from the sights and sounds of the surrounding world and from internal events such as hunger and digestion. At the same time, the baby makes all sorts of random movements, and certain movements become conditioned to follow certain stimuli. Eventually, the movements that produce no reward fade away, through extinction of the conditioned response. As the child grows, increasingly complex behaviors are conditioned, building up from the simpler ones.

Language

Watson believed that even human language was just a series of conditioned muscular responses in the lungs, larynx, throat, tongue, and lips. Eventually, the patterns associated with one word become connected to those of another, and words flow in their proper order. Meanwhile, words and phrases are conditioned responses to objects in the environment.

Thinking, Watson said, was a sequence of stimulus-response events in which the result of one connection acted as the stimulus for the next. Use of language was the result of conditioning that associated objects with words; thought was just a flow of unspoken words.

The teaching machine

The next major step forward in behaviorism resulted from the work of B. F. Skinner. Skinner introduced programmed instruction in a "teaching machine": a box with a window called a "frame" in which a small amount of information was displayed. After absorbing the information, his students were shown a question written in such a way that they almost always got the right answer. The satisfaction of giving the correct answer, Skinner said, served as a reinforcement to help students remember the material.

Skinner advocated a society in which conditioning was used to prevent and correct antisocial behavior. His ideas were widely applied to education. Teachers were taught that students needed grades and other incentives to perform to their maximum potential and that material should be carefully sequenced to condition related ideas to each other. Undesired behavior in the classroom was to be corrected by reinforcing positive behavior and eliminating the stimuli that triggered negative behavior.

Controversial issues

Behaviorism was widely criticized on both emotional and logical grounds. For one thing, behaviorists conducted most of their experiments on laboratory animals, and critics said it was unacceptable to assume that the results they obtained applied automatically to the more complex nervous systems of people.

Like Watson, Skinner believed that language was built entirely of conditioned responses connecting words to

Curriculum Context

Students might be asked to discuss Skinner's contribution to popularizing behaviorism.

objects and actions. Critics argued that individual differences in language learning meant there was also a genetic inherited component: that people learned language because they were prepared to form certain associations and not prepared for others. In other words, the organism itself was a part of the stimulus-response sequence, and thus not all behavior was determined simply by learning.

Behaviorism today

Today, most psychologists recognize that behaviorism opened a small window onto the human mind. Its first major contribution to psychology was methodology, or its way of doing science. The second was therapy, or a way of treating psychological problems.

Behavioral conditioning and modification

The behaviorists' focus on the relationship between events and behavior led them to explore whether undesirable behaviors could be changed. For instance, one of the goals of doctors in a psychiatric ward is to help the patients lead a normal life, and this often starts with basic tasks that address the patient's problems. In several cases these goals have been achieved by rewarding normal, healthy behaviors with tokens. In token systems patients receive immediate rewards for appropriate behaviors. Research showed that the introduction of a token economy had real, positive effects on the behavior of patients who had spent many years in the hospital. Token economies have also been used effectively to improve behavior in both mainstream and special needs schools.

Phobias
Extreme and irrational fears.

Behavioral methods have been shown to be effective in treating a wide range of problems, such as fear of spiders or anxiety about public speaking. The methods used to treat such phobias usually depend on the principle of a conditioned reflex. The patient is gradually exposed to mild versions of the thing feared, often accompanied by pleasurable stimuli. People with agoraphobia might begin by sitting on the front porch. Later they might move to the end of the front walk, and so on, until they can tolerate crowded public places.

Agoraphobia
Fear of going out in public.

Other researchers developed a more extreme approach called "aversion therapy." This approach attempted to correct bad habits by associating them with unpleasant stimuli, such as loud sounds and unpleasant smells. These techniques have been applied to alcohol and drug addiction and to obsessive-compulsive behavior.

The behaviorist legacy

The most significant contribution the behaviorists made to modern psychology is the one that is hardest to see. They insisted that psychology should be a science. Scientists perform carefully controlled experiments, and so should psychologists.

Obsessive-compulsive behavior
Behavior characterized by extreme anxiety and repetitive actions aimed at reducing that anxiety.

Out of Sight, Out of Mind?

If you were to travel to a neighboring town, you would no longer be able to see your house, but you would know that it was still there. For a long time many psychologists believed that infants could not grasp this fundamental concept. But the problem with trying to test theories about babies is that babies have difficulty interacting with people and objects in ways researchers can measure accurately. Psychologists get around this by using behaviorist techniques to test rats and pigeons.

Virtually all animals habituate (get used to repeated events). For example, the first time a blue light flashes in a rat's cage, the rat will turn to look at it. However, by the time the light has flashed perhaps 40 times, the rat ignores it. Habituation vanishes if something surprising happens: If a red light flashes, the blue-habituated rat will start to pay attention to the light again. This means the rat must be able to tell the difference between the red and blue lights.

Researchers have used the fact that surprise removes habituation to see whether babies find certain events surprising or not. For example, a baby will be repeatedly shown an event until she shows habituation. The event is then changed. If the baby starts looking again, she must be able to detect that change.

Neuropsychology

Neuropsychologists study the way in which the mental apparatus is organized in the brain, an area that only began to move from speculation to true science in the late 18th century, when researchers linked brain injury and loss of function.

How do we know that the brain is the organ of mental life? We know, for example, that four of our five external sense organs are located exclusively in the head, and even the simplest understanding of anatomy shows that the nerves from the sense organs travel toward the brain.

Although the brain seems an obvious place to look for the biological basis of the mind, the importance of the heart as the organ of the mind (especially in emotion) was the topic of a long-standing debate dating back to the philosophers of ancient Greece.

The influence of phrenology

Franz Gall (1758–1828) argued that different regions of the outer surface of the brain might be specialized for various personality traits, such as "destructiveness" and "veneration" (worship or respect). This argument came to be called phrenology. The doctrine of phrenology suggested that scientists could gauge a person's personality by feeling the skull for bumps. These bumps were thought to develop in particular places because the underlying brain regions responsible for particular faculties made an impression on the skull.

The study of deficit

Jean-Baptiste Bouilland (1796–1881) stressed the value of examining the brain itself (at autopsy) as evidence for inferring the importance of brain regions. Bouilland noticed that people who had suffered a stroke (caused by a loss of blood supply to a portion of the brain), and who had experienced language problems as a result,

Autopsy

An examination of a dead body to discover the cause of death or the extent of disease.

tended to have suffered their damage in the anterior (front) regions of the brain. This focus on function, rather than structure, was a significant advance in brain science.

Phineas Gage

Phineas Gage worked on the railroads of North America in the 1840s and was one of the most famous patients in neuropsychology. An explosion propelled a tamping rod through Gage's skull and the frontal lobe of his brain. Only a relatively small area of the frontal lobe was damaged. Gage made a rapid physical recovery, but he underwent some distinctive psychological changes as a result of his injury. Previously he had been the team foreman —a position of some responsibility— and was regarded as a reliable character. After the accident he became uninhibited and acted in socially inappropriate ways, making a series of bad decisions in his work and personal life. Toward the end of his life he worked as part of a traveling show, exhibiting himself and the rod that had passed through his brain.

We now know, from countless cases since Gage's, that damage to this part of the frontal lobes almost always leads to this particular type of personality change. Patients like Gage are unable to use their emotional experiences about the world to make decisions about the right and wrong things to do.

Jean-Martin Charcot (1825–1893) searched for the locations of neurological and nonneurological disorders. His approach was later called the "clinicoanatomical" method. The name derived from the fact that it involved comparing two separate classes of evidence: the clinical evidence of the patient's behavior and the anatomical evidence of the site of the patient's injury.

The best-known example of this sort of correlation comes from the work of Paul Broca (1824–1880). Broca concluded that the frontal lobe of the left hemisphere of the brain was specialized for language production, with other brain regions presumably specialized for other, yet to be discovered functions. Later, other researchers applied a similar logic to dozens of psychological functions in the brain.

Correlation
The relationship or connection between two or more things.

Hemisphere
One of the two halves—left and right—of the brain.

A century of discovery

In the late 1800s scientists realized that the outer surface (cortex) of the left hemisphere is involved in several language functions. Various aspects of language, such as production, repetition, and comprehension, all seem to have regions of specialization in the left hemisphere.

Later attention focused on the functions of the right hemisphere. We now know that this hemisphere is involved in other areas of speech, such as rhythm and melody, and in a range of spatial and attentional functions. In the 1960s Roger Sperry conducted a series of experiments on epileptic patients, who had all been treated by having their hemispheres surgically disconnected by cutting through the bundle of nerve fibers between them, called the corpus callosum. With the corpus callosum severed, each hemisphere seemed in some ways to act like a separate brain.

In the 1950s Brenda Milner was researching the effects of damage to the hippocampus when she discovered that people with this type of injury could not learn some types of new knowledge. Thus it appeared that the hippocampus was crucial for storing new information and for consolidating new memories.

Brain regions

Psychologists need to be cautious about how they interpret neuropsychological findings that might suggest that some areas in the brain are centers for face recognition, memory, or language. Making an intellectual leap like this requires several assumptions. One obvious problem is that we may be seeing an injury to just one part of a widespread network in the brain—one in which all of the parts perform the task of face memory, recognition, or language by their combined action. If a series of brain regions participate in a given process, then damage to any of them will

Epileptic
Suffering from epilepsy, a disorder marked by convulsions or periods of loss of consciousness.

Hippocampus
Part of the brain, thought to be the center of emotion, memory, and the autonomic nervous system.

disrupt a person's ability to do that task. Rather than focusing on "centers," researchers should seek to identify the different brain regions linked to a given function and understand their individual contributions. Much of the important work in neuropsychology has been in understanding the way in which several brain regions contribute to forming a functional system.

Wernicke's area

Broca's area

central sulcus

1. Prefrontal cortex
2. Olfactory cortex
3. Premotor cortex
4. Motor cortex
5. Sensory cortex
6. Sensory association cortex
7. Language cortex
8. Visual association cortex
9. Primary visual cortex
10. Auditory association cortex

The main functions of different parts of the cortex. The regions labeled 1–4 are part of the frontal lobes. Regions 5 to 8 are parts of the parietal lobes; 9 is the occipital lobe; and 10 is part of the temporal lobe. The motor cortex and the sensory cortex are also known as the precentral gyrus and the postcentral gyrus, for their positions on either side of the central sulcus.

The latest developments

During the 1970s and 1980s it became increasingly clear to some cognitive psychologists that neurological patients offer an excellent method for testing various theories of cognitive function. Before long the hybrid discipline of cognitive neuropsychology emerged. This new field involves both cognitive psychologists and neuropsychologists.

Technological changes have enabled scientists to observe brain activity in neurologically healthy subjects and to see which areas of the brain are active when a person is involved in a particular mental task.

Another change in neuropsychology began in the 1990s, with an increasing interest in the long-neglected issue of emotion. This has led to startling demonstrations of the role that emotions play in some aspects of cognition such as memory or language.

Brain-imaging Techniques

Brain-imaging began in the 1920s, when electric impulses from the human scalp were measured. Since then new and improved techniques for seeing the brain at work have helped doctors study brain disease and psychologists pinpoint precise areas of activity.

Several ground-breaking techniques have been invented that image the workings of the human brain. These techniques have also helped psychologists understand what is happening in the brains of people with mental disorders.

Curriculum Context

Some curricula ask students to compare the information about the brain that different imaging techniques provide.

There are several brain-imaging (also known as neuroimaging or functional imaging) techniques that can be used to study the human brain. All of these techniques are used to study the living human brain and to reveal abnormal brain patterns without surgery.

Electrical and magnetic fields

The human brain contains about 100 billion nerve cells called neurons, which connect to other nerve cells by means of long fiber. Like all cells in the body, neurons act like tiny batteries. There is a voltage difference (nearly one-tenth of a volt) between the inside and the outside of the cell, with the inside usually carrying a more negative charge. When a neuron is activated, positively charged sodium ions rush in through pores in the neuron's membrane, briefly reversing the voltage and causing the neuron to "fire" an impulse, or action potential.

Voltage difference

A difference in electrical potential.

The voltage changes inside active neurons produce tiny electrical fields that radiate through brain tissue, the skull, and the skin, and can be picked up through electrodes stuck to the surface of the scalp: This is an EEG recording. Magnetic fields accompanying the electrical fields also radiate through the skull, and they can be measured with sensitive magnetic field

EEG

Electroencephalography: the measurement of the brain's electrical activity.

detectors to produce an MEG recording. Both EEG and MEG require thousands of neurons to be active to detect a signal and produce an image.

Electroencephalography

Hans Berger was the first to measure electrical activity at the scalp. He used two large sheets of tin foil (which served as electrodes), placed them around his son's scalp, and recorded a rhythmic pattern of electrical activity arising from the boy's brain. This was the moment-by-moment electrical response of cells near the surface of the brain.

MEG
Magnetoencephalography: the measurement of the magnetic fields produced by the brain's electrical activity.

Electrode
The conductor through which electricity enters or leaves an object.

Hans Berger

Hans Berger (1873–1941) made many discoveries from EEG recordings. He found that brain waves oscillate at about 10 cycles per second when the eyes are closed and a person is relaxed. He named this pattern alpha waves. During a period of mental activity when the eyes are open, alpha waves are replaced by beta waves, which move faster. Berger found that alpha waves diminish during sleep, general anesthesia, and cocaine stimulation, and with brain injuries. Their frequency increases in epileptic patients. Later Berger recorded EEGs from infants, discovering that brain waves begin to appear at about two months of age. This corresponds to the time when brain neurons become sheathed in myelin, a substance critical to neural activity.

In the 1950s hospitals began to routinely use EEG to detect abnormalities in brain function caused by head injuries, brain tumors, infections in the brain, epileptic seizures, and sleep disorders. More recently, further technological advances have increased the ability of EEG to measure brain activity, and researchers can now record activity from the entire head simultaneously on a millisecond timescale.

In a typical EEG experiment many electrodes are stuck to a subject's scalp. The electrodes are made of a conductive metal, such as gold or tin, and are attached to the scalp in a coating of conductive gel (salt

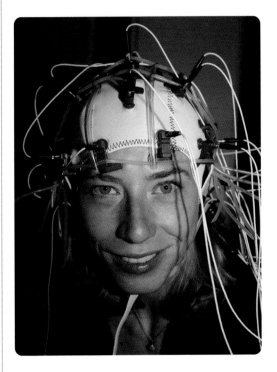

In an EEG scan electrodes—often embedded in a cap, as in this picture— are attached to the scalp. The electrodes detect brain activity by measuring electrical currents in the brain cells. This produces a continuing measure of activity over time, and the information is converted into images that can be displayed on a computer screen.

Visual cortex

The part of the brain dealing with sight.

solution), which maximizes the amount of electrical activity picked up. They feed into a sensitive amplifier that records the electrical impulses from each electrode. A computer then transforms these measurements into a scalp-shaped, multicolored image that can be displayed on screen. Different colors on the image indicate the different levels of electrical activity (neuronal firing) in the brain.

To investigate the areas of the brain activated by a particular psychological or sensory stimulus, psychologists often use EEG to record event-related potentials. EEG provides a constant measure of electrical activity in the brain, while an event-related potential (ERP) is an electrical response that occurs at a fixed time relative to a particular stimulus, such as a tone, a word, or an image (the event).

Magnetoencephalography (MEG)

The electric currents produced by brain activity generate tiny magnetic fields. If subjects are studied in a magnetically shielded room, it is possible to measure these fields using sensitive detectors—a technique called MEG. Measurements made in this way are called magnetoencephalograms (MEGs). In the first MEG experiment in 1975 subjects were presented with visual stimuli while scientists measured the magnetic fields on their scalps. The experiment showed that there were magnetic responses at the back of the brain, which is where the visual cortex lies. Since then MEG measurements have been used clinically to characterize the magnetic abnormalities that accompany a wide variety of brain diseases and to investigate the normal workings of the human brain.

Limits of EEG and MEG

Many discoveries involving the processing of sensory and cognitive processes have been reported using both EEG and MEG. Both methods have limits, however. First, EEG and MEG have a relatively low spatial resolution—they measure activity arising from several centimeters of brain tissue. Second, it is difficult to accurately localize the source of the electrical or magnetic activity arising from within the brain. Third, EEG and MEG measure activity mainly from the cortical regions: the areas of the brain that lie near the surface.

Measuring blood flow

When a population of neurons becomes activated, these cells require an increased flow of blood to replenish their supply of oxygen and glucose, which they depend on for energy. The main brain-imaging techniques that measure blood flow are positron emission tomography (PET) and functional magnetic resonance imaging (fMRI). The principle underlying them is the tight coupling of neuron activity with glucose and oxygen metabolism.

Positron emission tomography (PET)

The history of positron emission tomography (PET) dates back to the early 1950s. PET measures the volume and location of blood flow in the body by tracking radioactive chemicals (called "tracer chemicals") injected into the subject's bloodstream. These tracers emit positrons (minute particles with a positive charge), and a radiation detector camera surrounding the subject's head tracks where in the subject's brain the positrons are emitted.

Tracers can show blood flow, oxygen and glucose metabolism, or the location and concentrations of

Glucose
A sugar that is an important energy source in living organisms.

Metabolism
The chemical processes within an organism that maintain life.

Radioactive
Emitting ionizing radiation or particles.

drugs or naturally occurring brain chemicals (neurotransmitters) in the tissues of the working brain. High-powered computers then use the PET data to produce multicolored images that show where the blood flowed, which researchers use to study brain activity during different experimental tasks and conditions. The PET camera is capable of producing 3-D images, but researchers often show the areas of activation as 2-D "slices" so that it is possible to see exactly where in the brain the activation occurred. PET is used to detect abnormal blood flow in the brain.

CT Scanning

Computed tomography (also called CT scanning) is another diagnostic technique that combines the technology of X-rays and computers. It produces static, cross-sectional images of the brain or body, revealing structure but not function. The term tomography comes from the Greek word *tomos*, meaning "slice," and *graphia*, which means "describing." The technique was originally used to image the brain. During a scan patients pass through a doughnut-shaped scanner containing an X-ray tube and a detector, which rotate around them. Lead shutters focus the X-rays on a tissue thickness of 1–10 mm. During each 360-degree rotation the detector takes numerous profiles, or snapshots, of the X-ray beam which a computer combines to form a single 2-D image. The 2-D slices can be put together to create a 3-D image.

Magnetic resonance imaging (MRI)

Magnetic resonance imaging (MRI) uses a large magnetic field to produce high-quality, 3-D images of brain structure without the need for radioactive tracers. Researchers use a large cylindrical magnet to create a magnetic field around the subject's head and then send radio waves through the magnetic field. Different structures and tissues in the brain have different magnetic properties, and the radio waves make their component particles appear differently on the MRI image. A computer uses this information to construct an image. A single MRI scan produces many static 2-D "slices" of the brain, and by putting these slices

Radio waves

A form of low-frequency electromagnetic radiation that is used for long-distance communication.

together, a computer can produce a complete 3-D image of the brain, showing images of both surface and deep brain structures in great anatomical detail. MRI is used to detect minute changes in brain structure and to detect strokes, hemorrhages, and brain tumors.

In the 1980s and 1990s new techniques enabled scientists to use MRI to image the brain at work: functional magnetic resonance imaging (fMRI) measures the amount of oxygenated blood sent to particular regions in the brain.

Comparison of PET and fMRI

There are several advantages of fMRI over PET. First, fMRI does not expose subjects to ionizing radiation. Second, PET usually takes 40 seconds or longer to image brain activity, while an fMRI scan can produce images every second. Thus fMRI can show brain activity with greater precision than PET. Third, fMRI produces higher-quality images.

There are some disadvantages of fMRI. It is extremely loud, so the subject must wear earplugs, and it is more enclosed than the PET scanner, which can be a problem for claustrophobic people. Also, fMRI images can be contaminated by even a tiny head movement. PET can also identify which brain receptors are being activated by neurotransmitters, drugs, and chemicals, which is beyond the scope of fMRI.

Claustrophobic
Having an irrational fear of confined places.

Neurotransmitters
The chemicals that transfer impulses from one nerve fiber to another.

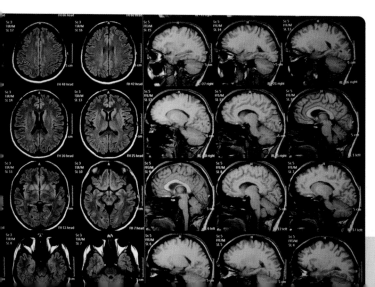

Magnetic resonance images (MRI) of a person's head. MRI scans show structures in the brain with a great deal of precision.

Cognitive Psychology

Cognitive psychology emerged in the late 1950s as researchers developed theories based on the idea of the mind as an information-processing device. They believed that stimulation received by the senses was transformed into some kind of internal representation that the mind could interpret, store, and act upon.

Artificial intelligence

The science of making machines that can think for themselves.

Curriculum Context

A student may be asked to outline the principles of cognitive psychology.

Cognitive psychology is closely tied to the study of the physiology of the brain and nervous system, and to the study of artificial intelligence (AI) in computers. Sometimes experimental cognitive psychology, physiological psychology, and the study of artificial intelligence are combined under the heading of cognitive science.

Cognitive psychologists divide thinking into separate processes, such as attention, perception, memory storage, memory recall, decision-making, and problem solving. The lines between these areas are hard to draw, and the different areas often interact.

The science of psychology began with philosophers of the late 19th century who carefully analyzed their own thought processes. In the early 1920s the behaviorists said that researchers should deal only with what could be directly observed and measured in the form of stimuli and responses, or behavior.

The cognitive revolution
In the early 1960s there was a build up to what some people called the cognitive revolution. The first factor that contributed to this return to an emphasis on cognition was the rise of the Gestalt school of psychology. Gestalt psychologists had showed through experiment that some perceptual patterns and structures possess more qualities as a whole than the sum of their individually considered parts.

Another influence on cognitive research began with discoveries in neurosurgery during World War II (1939–1945), when many people suffered head injuries that destroyed parts of their brains. Doctors examining these patients found that injuries to specific parts of the brain resulted in the loss of specific abilities.

Neurosurgery
Surgery performed on the brain or spinal cord.

Another development that occurred during the war was the emergence of the digital computer. Some researchers believed that if they could model thought processes on the way a computer worked, it might also help them understand how the mind worked.

Behaviorism and cognition

This return to the study of thought did not mean that psychologists rejected behaviorism entirely. Cognitive

Tower of Hanoi

French mathematician Edouard Lucas devised the Tower of Hanoi in 1833. He was inspired by the legend of the Hindu priests who were given a stack of 64 gold disks, each disk a little smaller than the one beneath it, and challenged to transfer them one by one from one of three poles to another, ensuring that no disk was ever placed on top of a smaller one. It was said that when they finished, the temple would crumble to dust, and the world would end.

To move the entire tower, the priests would have needed to make $2^{64}-1$ separate moves (18,446,744,073,709,551,615)! So if they had worked day and night, making one move every second, it would have taken them just over 580 billion years to finish the job.

A computer program, the General Problem Solver, possessed the logic to solve the Tower of Hanoi problem after being programmed with a few general rules.

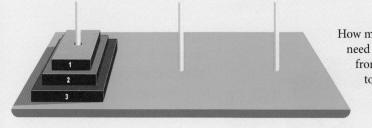

How many moves would you need to transfer the blocks from one of the three poles to another without ever placing a larger block on top of a smaller one?

psychologists also found ways to conduct rigorous objective experiments that measured outward behavior but revealed the inner workings of the mind. They also retained the behaviorists' insistence that all thought is carried out by physical mechanisms in the mind and nervous system.

While behaviorists had rejected any idea of mental imagery, cognitive psychologists proposed that thinking begins with the creation of a mental representation of an idea or perception, and that this is the basis for further processing. They assumed that, like a computer, the mind would break each process into a series of steps, and their research sought to find out what those steps might be.

Perception and attention

Perception is the process by which people interpret the stimuli that their sense organs report. As you read this book, your eyes report the page as a pattern of light and dark, but your brain separates the individual words and attaches meaning to them.

Studies of brain physiology show that tasks such as recognizing vertical and horizontal lines, identifying corners, and detecting motion seem to require the use of separate areas of the brain—thus some psychologists think it is likely that a great deal of processing takes place below conscious awareness. For example, some people with damage to the area of the brain that processes messages from the eye report a total lack of vision, and yet they are able to avoid obstacles of which they are not consciously

Driving requires a great deal of mental processing because the driver has to operate the vehicle and process numerous pieces of information about the roads and traffic. As the driver gains experience, much more of this processing takes place below the level of conscious awareness.

Top Down

In identifying what you see or hear, does the mind simply operate on the input until it finds sense or does it impose its own experience early on in the processing?

Top-down processing involves higher levels of consciousness from the beginning, such as when we draw on memory to identify the thing perceived.

The concept of top-down processing is demonstrated by experiments that show that context influences the things people perceive. People look at or listen to other things around the particular thing being perceived and apply their experience to help determine meaning.

In one experiment subjects heard one of the following:

The cobbler said that the *eel was still on the shoe.
The cook said that the *eel was still on the orange.
The projectionist said that the *eel was still on the projector.
The mechanic said that the *eel was still on the car.

In each case the asterisk represents a sound that was edited out of the recording and replaced with a cough. The researchers found that most subjects did not report that anything was missing. Instead, they reported that they heard the words *heel, peel, reel,* or *wheel* depending on which sentence they heard.

aware. In laboratory experiments people presented with stimuli so faint or brief as to be unaware of them can still make use of what they have not actively "seen."

When people see a book, how do they identify it as a book? A popular recognition theory is that people store a sort of general idea of a book, which psychologists call a "schema." The fact that people can recognize an object from a simple drawing representing the object provides evidence for this theory. For example, a circle, two dots, and an arc in the proper arrangement are enough to indicate a face.

Another theory proposes that what people store is not an image but a list of features. A book, for example, is identified by the fact that it is rectangular, has printing on the spine, and so on. This approach works well in explaining why people can recognize a letter of the alphabet when it is presented in many different sizes or printing fonts.

Curriculum Context

Students may find it useful to understand theories of perception in cognitive psychology.

Memory

Adding new information or experiences to your mental supply, storing information, and retrieving information when you need it are all aspects of memory. Evidence exists for at least three types of storage: The first is a sort of buffer that holds relatively unprocessed visual and audio data from the sense organs; second is the working or short-term memory, which holds a limited amount of information for a few seconds; and last is long-term memory, which is stored more or less permanently.

Some psychologists believe that the transfer of information from working memory to long-term storage is the result of attention and rehearsal. Other researchers suggest that linking new information with previously stored data is the key to long-term storage, while others argue that long-term and working storage occur together. Cognitive psychologists usually test these theories in the laboratory by presenting subjects with lists of words to memorize under various conditions.

Once information is stored in long-term memory, how is it then retrieved? Different processes seem to be involved, depending on whether the task is to recognize the information or to recall it from scratch. An example of a recognition task would be seeing a name in a list and realizing you had met the person with that name. A recall task would require you to remember the name without any cues. In the first case you presumably search your memory supply for the presented stimulus and then retrieve whatever information is stored along with it. In the recall task you might come up with candidates, and you would have to test each one to see if it fitted the definition.

Experiments have shown that people can generate only a limited number of candidates at one time, which

Buffer

In computing, an area of temporary memory.

Curriculum Context

Students should be able to explain theories about the ways in which memories are stored in the brain.

means that when they are searching for a word, they probably do not search sequentially through all of the thousands of words they know. Researchers found that subjects who could not quite remember the word were helped when given the first letter, which narrowed the possibilities available.

Language

Cognitive psychologists also try to understand the mechanisms by which people produce and understand language. Common theories suggest that there are several distinct steps in speech production. First, the speaker organizes the concepts to be presented; then the grammatical structure of the sentence is mentally laid out; and finally, individual words are added into the structure. Understanding is thought to follow a similar series of steps. Theories vary as to the number and complexity of these steps, but experiments have shown that speakers do plan ahead.

The greater the angle of rotation between two figures, the longer it takes for people to decide whether the shape on the left is identical to the one on the right. This means that you are probably mentally rotating the image to find a match and not examining abstract knowledge to decide which shape is identical to the other.

Problems and decisions

All the different processes discussed so far—perception, memory, and language—come together in problem solving and decision making. Research by cognitive psychologists has focused on factors that prevent problem solving.

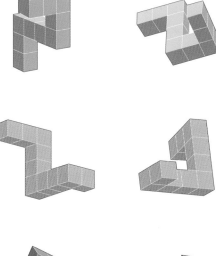

In typical experiments cognitive researchers present subjects with simple logical statements and ask them to draw conclusions. While ideal logic might dictate a certain answer, subjects will not always choose it, but may be distracted by irrelevant information.

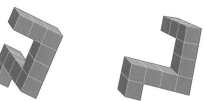

Researchers have also studied the ways in which superior problem solvers differ from other people. Chess masters were found to

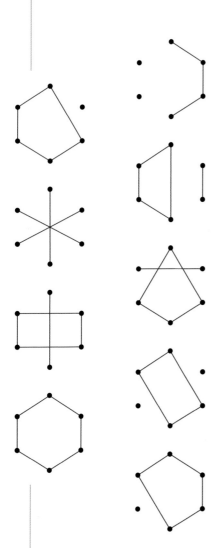

consider fewer possible moves than less gifted players, but those they did consider were all good ones. Their superior performance seemed to result from a large memory of possible games and an efficient system for sorting through these memories.

Thus problem solving and decision making seem to parallel the mechanism of memory recall: Possible solutions to a problem or possible outcomes of a decision are generated and then compared with the desired outcome.

Evolutionary theory
In 1983 Jerry Fodor suggested that the mind might be constructed from a variety of specialized information-processing devices, or modules. In the same year Howard Gardner proposed that there were eight separate intelligences, each of which was associated with a different cognitive module.

One of the most extreme positions of all on modularity was proposed by Leda Cosmides and John Tooby in the early 1990s. They argued that the human mind evolved to solve problems that recurred in every generation, threatening survival and reproduction. They believed that the mind evolved different modules for solving different adaptive problems.

Individual dots are meaningless; but when they are connected, they form recognizable patterns, as the shapes above show. In the same way, knowledge is not stored in the neurons of the brain but in the patterns of connections between them.

Much cognitive psychology concentrates on the cognitive activities and processes that go on in the mind. Generally it is taken for granted that at a simpler or lower level these processes are implemented by the interaction of the brain's neurons. David Marr

(1945–1980) argued that to understand cognition, we must understand the principles and laws governing complex mental activity.

John R. Anderson (born 1947) contended that researchers should begin by assuming that human behavior was evolutionarily adapted to the environment. Essentially, they need to describe the nature of the environment in which behavior takes place.

Environment

The surroundings or conditions in which an animal lives.

Viewing the brain's activities
A complete theory of cognition must understand the information-processing mechanism that solves that problem. Like a tool, that information-processing mechanism must be embodied in a physical thing. For people and other animals that thing is the brain.

Developments in medical technology mean that scientists can now examine the structure and activity of the brain. Brain-imaging techniques enable psychologists to study people's brains while they are engaged in certain kinds of behavior, such as dreaming, and associate these behaviors with particular forms of brain activity. For example, scanning techniques have been used to shed light on mental representation.

The application of cognitive science
Research in cognitive science has many practical applications, including computer programming. Studies of perception can aid in the treatment of dyslexia and other perceptual disorders, and can help in the design of everything from road signs to living spaces, while a better understanding of learning and memory contributes to teaching. But basic cognitive research continues to seek simply a better understanding of how the mind works, with a particular focus on consciousness.

Dyslexia

A disorder that involves difficulty in learning to read without affecting general intelligence.

Psycholinguistics

What could be simpler than speaking or understanding speech? Almost all of us do it every day, using words to communicate our ideas without any real effort. But how do we acquire language? Psycholinguistics studies how people learn and use language.

Ancient Greek philosophers wondered why objects were named the way they were. They discussed whether word names were randomly assigned to objects by some greater power, or whether they were chosen to fit their meaning or shape. There was also great interest in the rules that people used to assemble words into sentences. We now call these rules grammar or syntax. Such rules allow us to understand the ideas that others want to convey.

The first dictionaries did not appear until the Middle Ages. They remain important to modern linguists because they contain a wealth of information about the languages spoken and written at that time, and also about the way in which invaders assimilated foreign languages, and how languages evolved into their present form.

Assimilate
To integrate into something else.

Words without frontiers

During the 15th and 16th centuries the invention and development of the printing press meant that books could be produced inexpensively and distributed in large numbers. At the same time, the first academies emerged in which thinkers and philosophers gathered to talk about the origin of languages.

People became more and more interested in the dynamic aspects of language—how it is represented in our minds, how we comprehend it, and how we learn it—and by the early 20th century this interest had led to the birth of psycholinguistics.

In 1957 Noam Chomsky distinguished between the notions of competence and performance. Competence is the idealized knowledge that we have of our own language, most of which is expressed in terms of grammatical rules. Performance refers to the actual use of competence in real-life situations. Psycholinguistics is concerned with explicit language behavior, describing how we use language to communicate our ideas with each other.

Comprehending language

According to Chomsky, we comprehend speech by matching the language performance of another person to our own language competence. During the 1970s psycholinguists tested Chomsky's theory, devising a range of language experiments from which they gathered data. The availability of computers helped them collect vast amounts of information about the competence and speed with which people recognize speech, and the results of their experiments were as follows.

When we listen to speech, we recognize four or five words per second and dozens of sentences every minute. However, language comprehension is not simple and straightforward.

Curriculum Context

Students should be aware of Chomsky's views on language performance.

Human speech is the result of a complex chain of operations that involves conceptualization, formulation, and articulation. Our accompanying gestures and the tone we adopt may also alter the meaning of what we say.

First, we need to recognize the individual speech sounds (phonemes). This stage can be problematic because people pronounce phonemes differently depending on their accent, age, health, and mood.

Curriculum Context

Students should be able to identify the basic units of language and explain how they are combined.

The second step consists of segmenting the string of phonemes into distinct words. Speech segmentation is necessary because speech typically contains no gaps or pauses. Speech segmentation allows successful recognition of the words used. Once this process has been successfully completed, we have accessed the representations of the words in our "mental lexicon" (the personal dictionary housed in our brains that contains all the words we know).

The final step consists of making sense of the words or accessing what they mean. The meaning of each word is retrieved from our knowledge system and interpreted in the context of the sentence.

How Do We Know All This?

The study of the dynamic aspects of language (how processing stages interact with each other) requires ingenious and indirect techniques. One of the most popular consists of measuring reaction times. It is thought that a mental operation, such as recognizing a word, takes longer if it involves many steps than if it involves only a few. Thus it takes longer to recognize an infrequent word, such as "scalp," than a frequent one, such as "school," because, presumably, words are looked up by order of frequency. To measure reaction times, participants sit in a quiet room and listen to speech over headphones or read material on a computer monitor. They are instructed to perform a task—for example, to detect a certain sound or decide if what they hear is a word—as fast as they can. A computer measures how long it takes them to push the button. Reaction time differences can be as small as 15 or 20 milliseconds (one-fiftieth of a second).

The sequence of events described above takes place in less than half a second and seems easy to us. That is because we have learned to make our mental processes more and more automatic over years of practice. Because we recognize words effortlessly, we can devote our attention to other tasks, such as thinking and planning responses.

Accessing the mental lexicon

At birth we all start out with an empty mental lexicon. This memory store of words grows quickly in the first years of life, from 100 words at around one year to about 50,000 words in adulthood. When we hear speech, we recognize each word almost immediately, accessing the right word in our mental lexicon in less than half a second.

Speech production

Speaking begins with an idea that we want to express. Thoughts are translated into concepts that can be expressed in words. Once the conceptual structure of the message is ready, we then need to retrieve the right words from our mental lexicon. We also want the words to be assembled into a syntactically correct and meaningful sentence. The result of this "formulating" stage is not yet real speech. It is internal speech—the silent voice you hear inside your head when you think.

We are now ready to voice the internal speech. Our lungs, larynx, tongue, nose, and lips collaborate to produce a clear and audible sentence. This stage is termed articulation because it involves the muscular programs necessary to utter the words.

Articulation
The formation of clear and distinct sounds in speech.

Fortunately, people accomplish the above operations very quickly. Speech production is not as easy and automatic as speech comprehension, however. People differ greatly in how well they speak and how swiftly they can articulate ideas.

Language development

People have wondered for hundreds of years how we acquire language. The Mughal emperor of India, Akbar

(1542–1605), believed that people acquired language by hearing others speak. To test his hypothesis, he confined several newborn babies to a mansion isolated from civilization and guarded by mute nurses. Four years later he returned and found that the children could not emit a single speech sound.

There have also been many reports of wild or isolated children who have experienced years of language deprivation and consequently never learn more than a few words. And if they are able to learn words, they usually cannot master the rules of grammar. Recovery seems to depend on the age at which language learning began.

For most of us language acquisition comes naturally, beginning early in life and requiring almost no formal training. Contemporary psycholinguists divide this learning process into several stages.

Mother tongue

People learn the typical intonation of their native language before they are born. From inside the womb a fetus can hear the low frequencies of its mother's voice and the voices of people close by. Once born, infants will show a preference for the voices of the people who spent a lot of time near their mother during pregnancy. They also show a clear preference for what is known as their mother tongue.

In the first few months of life infants become familiar with the speech sounds of their environment. At around six months they understand a few words, usually those that occur often in their environment. By the time they reach their first birthday they usually have a large repertoire of phonemes and a few true words. These first words may be difficult to understand and words do not yet have a clear meaning.

Curriculum Context

Case studies of isolated people or "wild" children brought up without human company are useful in understanding language development.

Intonation

The rise and fall of the voice in speaking.

The two-word stage occurs at the end of the second year and coincides with a sharp rise in the number of words children know. With a few hundred words in their vocabulary it becomes easier to express ideas, but many two-word sentences are still ambiguous.

Only at the syntactic stage, at around two and a half years, do children start saying real sentences. They contain verbs, prepositions, adverbs, and so on, and follow syntactical rules. This is when children learn the importance of word order in sentences.

Language in the Brain

Paul Broca (1824–1880) first established that in most people the areas of the brain that control language comprehension and production are located in the left hemisphere, behind the left ear. Carl Wernicke (1848–1905) discovered that damage in an area slightly farther back from Broca's area was responsible for difficulty in comprehending speech.

Neurolinguistic researchers are trying to identify the exact location of the mental lexicon and the area of the brain that controls syntax. An accurate model of language processing in the brain would help surgeons during operations on the brain.

Curriculum Context

Students may be asked to trace the stages of language development from infancy to childhood.

Research shows that we start to learn our native language while we are still in our mother's womb.

Computer Simulation

One important reason for the so-called cognitive revolution in psychology during the 1950s and 1960s was the development of the computer. The computer soon became a valuable research tool, enabling psychologists to create programs and systems that tried to simulate human brain activity and mental processes.

Microchip

A tiny wafer of semiconducting material used to make an integrated circuit.

Both the mind and the computer are information-processing systems that can read, output, store, and compare symbols. The mind uses nerve cells to carry out such tasks, while the computer completes these processes using microchips—but there are parallels in the way they work. Consequently psychologists can test their theories of what goes on in the mind by writing computer programs to simulate the way they think mental processes work. If the computer's output matches the performance of the people, it suggests that the way the computer solves the problem may be the way a person would go about the task.

The Turing Test

British mathematician and computer scientist Alan Turing (1912–1954) suggested the following test for artificial intelligence: Let a person have a conversation by typing at a console. In the next room, out of sight, are a person and a computer, and the tester will converse with both of them without being told which is which. If the tester cannot tell the difference, the computer can be said to be intelligent.

Many modern computer programs can hold a fairly acceptable conversation but none have been totally convincing.

The logic theorist

One of the earliest efforts to create a program that would simulate human thought was called the Logic Theorist. Developed in the 1950s, it used symbolic logic—a system for writing logical statements in the form of variables related by operators (link words such as AND, OR, and NOT). These relationships are naturally built into the architecture of a digital computer, which operates by using electronic "gates" that either conduct or do not conduct current.

The Logic Theorist was given a few axioms, a series of rules for performing logical operations on these axioms, and a mathematical theorem to prove. Logical operations governed by rules are called operators. By applying operators to the axioms, the Logic Theorist generated new statements in sequence until the result matched the theorem it had set out to prove. In this way it produced proofs of several theorems.

A new logic theory

Herbert Simon (1916–2001) conducted extensive studies of people solving similar logic problems while "thinking aloud," and his analysis convinced him that their thought processes were very different from the procedure used by the Logic Theorist.

Simon developed a new theory to describe problem solving. The problem solver, he said, began by creating a mental representation of the problem called the problem space, which might or might not contain all the elements needed to solve the problem. In this space would be a representation of the starting conditions (the way things were), the goal (the way things would be if the problem were solved), and a set of operators that the solver could apply.

Thus problems were solved by applying operators to the initial object until it could be changed into the desired final object. Sometimes the change could not be accomplished directly and had to be divided into various subtasks.

Scientists developed a computer program called the General Problem Solver (GPS) based on this research. GPS treated the initial situation and the goal as objects

Axiom

A statement or proposition accepted as true.

Theorem

A general proposition proved by a chain of reasoning.

and began by measuring the difference between them, before looking for an operator to reduce the difference.

Allen Newell (1927–1992) created a program called SOAR (an acronym of "Start, Objects, and Response"). SOAR is capable of learning as it goes along by a process known as "chunking." In human terms chunking occurs when we gather several pieces of information together into something we can think about and remember as a single item.

Processing approaches

All of the computer programs described so far use "symbol-processing" methods. Objects or ideas in the real world are represented by symbols that the computer manipulates, usually serially—that is, one part of the program performs an operation then passes the results on to another. Critics, however, argue that the brain probably does not work in this way.

Connectionism

Even in the 1950s physiologists believed the brain was a vast parallel processing system, and research since then has tended to confirm this hypothesis. Memories are stored and thought processes carried out by establishing complex patterns of connections among the neurons. These connections are not established instantly, in the way that an electronic switch opens and closes in a computer, but seem to be formed by repetition. If a neuron fires repeatedly, it eventually causes a nearby neuron to fire. A chemical change then takes place that lowers the resistance between the two neurons. As a result the second neuron will now fire at the same time as the first one.

In the 1950s scientists created what became known as artificial neural networks: systems that simulated the physiology of the brain, rather than its thought processes. This approach is known as connectionism

Parallel processing

The ability to carry out several tasks simultaneously.

Neurons

Brain cells specialized to conduct nerve impulses.

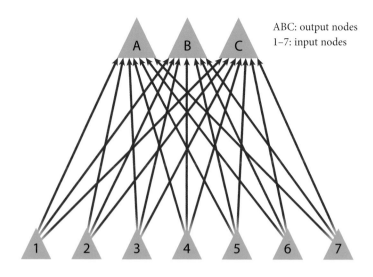

ABC: output nodes
1–7: input nodes

A simple illustration of a neural network. The signals sent by the numbered input nodes are "weighted" according to their distance from the three output nodes. Thus node 2 sends strong signals to node A, medium signals to node B, and weak signals to node C. The output nodes fire depending on the total amount of signal they receive. For example, a few signals from 3, 4, or 5 might cause B to fire or many signals from nodes 1 and 7. In this way the system can learn repeated patterns even if they are not identical.

because it emphasizes the connections between a situation and a response.

In its simplest form an artificial neural network consists of several input nodes connected to some output nodes. There may or may not be intermediate layers between them. Usually, each input node is connected to several nodes in an adjoining layer. When a stimulus activates an input node, a signal is sent to every node to which it is connected. But the signals are weighted—their effect diminishes as they reach nodes farther away. There are two types of neural network: supervised and unsupervised. In a supervised network the operator adjusts the weightings. In an unsupervised network the system adjusts its own weightings, a process known in other contexts as "learning."

Node
A point at which several pathways intersect or branch.

Current approaches
Today neural networks are used widely in pattern-recognition applications, such as optical character and speech recognition, and in "optimization" problems in which the goal is to find the most economical or efficient combination of interacting variables.

Evolutionary Psychology

Evolutionary psychology is one of the most recent approaches to the study of behavior, in which researchers combine a knowledge of biology and the history of our species to develop new ideas about human nature.

The publication in 1859 of Charles Darwin's (1809–1882) book *On the Origin of Species* revolutionized people's understanding of the natural world. Darwin's idea was relatively simple. Observing that some organisms seemed to reproduce more successfully than others, he assumed that some of these reproductive differences were the result of differences in the individuals' inherited traits. Environmental forces "selected" certain traits. Individuals with these traits were then more likely to survive, reproduce, and pass these traits to their offspring. Thus differences that led to greater reproductive success were passed down from one generation to the next. They spread throughout a population as individuals with the more successful traits in each generation out-reproduced individuals with less successful traits. This simple idea explains why organisms seem so well-adapted to survive and reproduce in their environments.

To test his theory, Darwin bred pigeons using artificial (as opposed to natural) selection methods, mating birds with desired traits to produce each subsequent generation. In this way he established that specific traits could be passed down from parent to offspring, although he did not understand the mechanism that enabled this. That was because he did not yet know about genes, the microscopic units of information found in the nucleus of cells.

Dawkins and the selfish gene

Darwin believed that the key to the evolutionary process lay in the number of surviving offspring that

---

Curriculum Context

Students should be able to explain how the environment influences evolutionary changes.

Gene

A unit of heredity that determines some specific characteristic and that is passed from parent to offspring.

each individual produced. Richard Dawkins (born 1941) disputed this, arguing that it was what happened to different genes, rather than to different individuals, that was crucial to understanding evolution. Although all individual organisms died, genes were "immortal" in the sense that their copies traveled from generation to generation.

William D. Hamilton (1936–2000) supported this theory. Hamilton knew that in some species of insect, colonies included many nonreproductive individuals that left no offspring at all. Hamilton pointed out that more of these individuals' genes survive in their sisters than would be the case in any offspring they had of their own. Thus in evolutionary terms it is better for them to help the queen reproduce than do so themselves.

Family Violence

Psychologists Martin Daly and Margo Wilson studied family violence. In 1988 they published *Homicide,* which took an evolutionary approach to violence, particularly in the context of family. Starting from the theory of kin selection, they predicted that parents' biological children would be less likely to be abused than nonbiological (adopted or step-) children. After combing through a wide range of historical and anthropological records, they reached some startling conclusions. They found that in the United States and Canada stepchildren were more than 50 times as likely to be fatally abused by their parents than biological children.

Evolution and humans

Several scientists have attempted to use evolutionary theory to understand human behavior. From their work a new field called evolutionary psychology has emerged, which is now recognized as a scientific discipline. Evolutionary psychology applies a modern understanding of the evolutionary principles of natural selection to human behavior and to the organ that generates this behavior, the human brain.

Curriculum Context

It may be useful to summarize the basic principles of evolutionary psychology.

Many evolutionary psychologists view the brain as an information-processing device much like a computer. Thus they see the brain as an organ that takes information from the various senses, processes it, and then produces behaviorial responses.

One important task of psychology is to identify the programs that constitute the brain's circuitry. Programs in the brain are products of evolution by natural selection, and this provides important clues to understanding the brain's circuits, or pathways.

Adaptations

According to Darwinian theory, the process of evolution preserves genes that enable individuals to perform tasks that promote survival and reproduction. These tasks—such as finding food, avoiding predators, and so on—are called "adaptive problems." Thus an adaptive problem is any difficulty faced by a species that has affected its reproductive success.

Because natural selection is a slow process, often requiring hundreds or thousands of generations for significant changes to occur, the only adaptive problems that matter are those that a given species faces repeatedly during its evolutionary history. This suggests that the programs that constitute human

A surfer rides a wave in Hawaii. Although this specific behavior is not a product of evolution, the skills required, such as balance and physical coordination, have evolved over many hundreds of generations. Evolution, therefore, has many unexpected outcomes.

psychology evolved because they helped our ancestors solve problems during human evolutionary history.

In his book *Adaptation and Natural Selection* (1966) biologist George C. Williams (born 1926) argued that evolution occurred because the traits of some organisms worked better than those of others. Over time the traits that functioned more efficiently in solving specific adaptive problems were selected over others, so an organism became better at performing the required functions. Such traits (the parts of organisms that are filtered by natural selection to perform specific, vital tasks) are called adaptations.

Curriculum Context

Students should be able to describe examples of evolutionary changes in animals other than humans.

Domain specificity

Domain specificity is the idea that evolution tends to create organisms with different parts, each designed to solve a particular problem. For example, birds have wings designed for flight, and fish have fins designed for an aquatic lifestyle.

Evolutionary psychologists believe that human brains develop along the same lines and for the same reason. Pathways in the brain must be able to solve different kinds of problems, and the problems that they solve are information-processing problems. They also believe that the brain consists of specialized pathways at every level. Their central premise is that the brain consists of a vast number of these specialized pathways that solve the adaptive problems faced by our ancestors during human evolutionary history: finding food, avoiding predators, hunting, attracting mates, and so on.

Learning

Throughout history people tended to believe that behavior was caused either by instinct (biology, or nature) or by learning (culture, or nurture). Evolutionary psychologists, however, believe that every aspect of an organism is produced by the interaction between its genes and the environment.

Language learning illustrates this idea. Babies cannot speak a language when they are born, but acquire it by listening to and interacting with the adults in their lives. However, they are equipped to learn language through an innate cognitive system that is adapted to the purpose. Steven Pinker (born 1954) referred to this capacity as an instinct—suggesting that the specific cognitive capacity for learning language evolved over the course of human history.

Curriculum Context

Students are expected to understand how evolutionary theory affects contemporary learning theories.

Evolutionary psychologists regard evolution as a process that adds more "instincts to learn," and that these extra mechanisms allow organisms greater flexibility. This approach suggests that learning mechanisms are likely to be related to a specific function of the brain.

Mating

A prominent example of research in evolutionary psychology is David Buss's work on human mating, which began with ideas from evolutionary theory. The first of them is that in species like humans in which females usually provide parental care, males can increase their reproductive success by mating with many females. Mating with multiple males will not lead to more offspring for females, however. This concept led Buss to suspect that males had evolved preferences for mating with multiple females. A second factor important to reproductive success in human males is the age of the female with whom the male mates. As a woman gets older, the number of children she may produce in the future decreases. Thus Buss hypothesized that men would have evolved a preference for younger women. Finally, Buss considered the preferences that evolutionary theory would predict for women. He reasoned that

People may not consciously choose a mate on the basis of reproductive potential or their ability to acquire resources, but research has shown that evolutionarily driven requirements such as these do play a major role in our selection of a mate.

an important mating factor for women would be the quantity of resources that a man could invest in his offspring and predicted that females would prefer males who displayed a greater ability to acquire these resources.

Buss tested his hypotheses by surveying thousands of subjects in 37 different cultures. He gave his subjects questionnaires that asked them about their preferences in mates. This collection of cross-cultural data generated strong support for his evolutionary hypotheses, showing that differences between the sexes in mating preferences are remarkably consistent across many cultures.

Cross-cultural
Relating to different cultures or comparison between them.

Criticisms

Evolutionary psychologists have been criticized for creating hypotheses that cannot be tested and are therefore unscientific. However, many research programs show that evolutionary theory can be tested using scientific principles.

Finally, some people believe that the theories of evolutionary psychology imply genetic determinism. In reality, however, the evolutionary view holds that behavioral adaptations, created by genes, lead to flexible behavior.

Genetic determinism
The idea that behavior is inflexible because it is totally determined by genetic influence.

Nonwestern Theories of the Mind

Current psychological theories and research projects are deeply rooted in Western culture. However, people in other cultures have also produced theories about psychological questions—and many of them have a much longer history than Western theories.

In both nonwestern countries and the Western world, researchers have recently begun to promote the study of so-called indigenous psychologies. An indigenous psychology is formulated along Western lines, integrating Western standards about research methodology and data analysis, but attempts to take account of cultural norms and values. Indigenous psychologies do not always allow for a proper appreciation of truly "homegrown" ideas.

Curriculum Context

It is important to understand the basic cultural differences between indigenous and endogenous psychologies.

Endogenous psychologies

An endogenous psychology, on the other hand, does not rely on Western models and research methods. All psychological ideas come from inside the community and, in most cases, have been part of the culture for thousands of years. Endogenous psychologies are often so strongly linked with folklore and cultural rites that they cannot be separated from religion, spirituality, and art. Many endogenous psychologies may not be taught in published writings, but through oral tradition, kept alive by the tales and myths that people share during family gatherings and religious ceremonies.

The Western concept of self

In Western psychologies the notion of the "self" usually refers to the individual person; it does not mean the same thing as personality. Western psychologists have unraveled the self into a whole series of subselves, such as the bodily self (our awareness of our body), the social self (how we present ourselves to others), the ideal self (the individual we would like to be), and the self-concept (the way we think about ourselves).

The definition of the self as a unity, the psychological distinctions between the self and the nonself, and the distinctions between bodily self and self-concept have been developed by Western psychologists studying Western people in Western cultures. In nonwestern cultures few of these definitions and distinctions apply.

An Asian person would probably find Western psychologies of the self bizarre for at least two reasons. First, Asian thought does not always distinguish between the self and the nonself, between what is part of ourselves and what belongs to the outside world. In the *Mandukaya Upanishad*, one of the most important philosophical books of Hinduism, the self is described as a synthesis between the subjective and the objective. This means that the self is not opposed to the outside world (the nonself, the objective), but is a combination of an individual's private experiences (the subjective) and the community in which he or she lives. The second reason why an Asian person would probably find Western ideas about the self strange is that in much eastern thought there is no distinction between the mind and the body.

Hinduism
A major and ancient religion and culture of the Indian subcontinent.

Until the 1940s most Western researchers believed that endogenous ideas were inferior to Western views and that they reflected an underdeveloped and primitive way of thinking. The work of social anthropologists such as Claude Lévi-Strauss (1908–2009) proved that this was a misguided

In Asian cultures psychology is strongly related to religion and spirituality. This Buddhist monk is meditating.

interpretation. After extensive fieldwork in Brazil and among Native American communities Lévi-Strauss concluded that the notion of the primitive mind was a myth. In a nonindustrialized society systems of thought are often much more complex than those adopted in the developed world.

Buddhist theory of emotion

Even concepts of emotion vary outside Western society, and one such example occurs in Buddhist cultures. Although there are different schools of Buddhism, the Buddhist tradition generally refers to a basic list of primary mental events called *kleshas*. A *klesha* is similar to an extreme affect, passion, or emotional reaction.

The six primary *kleshas* are pride, anger, desire, doubt, ignorance, and mistaken views—and they always emerge in response to a mental disturbance. So when people experience one or more of the six *kleshas*, they suffer from a deficiency in personality. According to the Buddhist psychology of emotions, *kleshas* require treatment and must be addressed by meditation and spiritual reflection.

Looking at the Buddhist theory of emotions from a Western viewpoint, the list of *kleshas* seems to include mental events that would never be described as emotions within Western psychology. Western psychologists, for example, would probably classify ignorance and doubt as cognitive states rather than emotional experiences. They would be unlikely to regard the *kleshas* as signs of a mental disturbance requiring treatment unless they became compulsive or extreme.

The Indian tradition

India also has a rich intellectual tradition concerning the origin and nature of emotions. Unlike Western psychologies, however, Indian ideas did not rely on the

Buddhism

An Asian religion founded by Siddartha Gautama in the fifth century B.C.

Meditation

Focusing one's mind or thinking deeply for a long period for spiritual purposes or for relaxation.

Cognitive states

Mental events related to thinking.

results of experiments, but came from reflections on religion, philosophy, and art. The oldest Indian theory of emotion is the *rasa* theory, which distinguishes between 8 aesthetic moods, 8 major emotions, and 33 minor emotions.

Some of the major aesthetic moods in the *rasa* tradition, such as love and horror, are immediately recognizable as important emotions within Western culture, while others, such as pathos and marvel, would be unlikely to enter a Western classification of emotions. The major aesthetic moods may also be expressed in very different ways from those seen in the United States and Europe. One of the *rasa* moods is horror, which is universally understood as an emotion, but a Westerner might not recognize it as expressed in an Indian drama. This contrast between expressions of similar emotions makes it clear that emotional expression is influenced by social customs and by biological factors.

An example from Africa

In a book called *Casting out Anger* Grace Harris describes how people of the Taita community in Kenya

Aesthetic
Concerned with beauty or the appreciation of it.

Pathos
A quality evoking sadness or pity.

The Rasa Tradition

The Sanskrit term *rasa*, meaning "aesthetic relish," refers to the theory of emotions developed by the Brahman sage and priest Bharata sometime between the fifth century B.C. and the second century A.D. Bharata discussed the key principles of *rasa* in the *Natyasastra*, a book concerned mainly with the art of performance, the theory of staged drama, and the techniques of acting.

The eight basic *rasas* in Bharata's work are primarily "aesthetic moods." He distinguished between love, comedy, pathos, fury, heroism, horror, hatred, and marvel, and linked each of these *rasas* with a major durable emotion: respectively, erotic feeling, mirth, sorrow, anger, energy/mastery, fear, disgust, and astonishment.

Alongside the major emotions Bharata listed 33 minor emotions, such as despair, pride, jealousy, and indignation. He believed that they were minor because they were less durable and did not occur in nonhuman animals.

think about the nature of emotions, and anger in particular. Good emotions are those that contribute to the survival of the individual and the community, while bad emotions lead to the destruction of the individual and his social relationships. The Taita believe that anger, which they call the "angry heart," is a bad emotion, and they try to replace it with a good emotion whenever it occurs. The Taita do this by performing purification rituals in which the affected individuals are relieved from the bad emotions they are enduring, and good emotions are restored.

Therapy

The word *therapy* is derived from the Greek *therapeia*, which means service, worship, religion, care, and healing. The original meanings make it clear that for the ancient Greeks treatment could take place within various contexts: magical, religious, or scientific.

Nonwestern communities still rely on treatment processes with a philosophical or religious basis. Chinese medicine, for example, is based on the Taoist vision of a universe ruled by two equal but opposite forces, yin and yang. Yin is passive and reflective, while

Yoga

The technique of yoga is one of the six systems of Indian philosophy. Yoga practitioners (yogis) have to learn to control the body-mind by canceling all thoughts and feelings, and when this is achieved, consciousness becomes empty and pure.

Yogis try to reach this state of purity through moral and physical discipline. As part of the moral discipline they have to abstain from violence and any type of sexual activity. For the physical discipline a specific posture and a particular type of breathing are important. Seated with their hands on their legs or knees, yogis keep their chin parallel to the ground and close their eyes. Then they concentrate on a point between their eyebrows and control their breathing until it becomes deep, regular, and slow. In this way yogis may reach the state of pure consciousness, where the distinction between self and nonself disappears, and the mental world merges with the physical world.

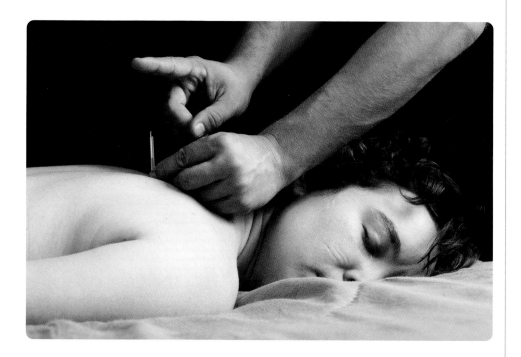

Acupuncture is a popular Chinese therapy. It involves inserting hot or cold needles at key points along the body's meridians: channels through which the body's energy (chi) is thought to circulate. Acupuncture frees the chi, balancing the yin and yang.

yang is active and dynamic. Illness is the result of an imbalance of the two forces within the body.

Chinese medicine practitioners must consider the patient as a whole, taking the state of body, mind, and spirit into account. Treatments might include diet, herbs, exercises such as tai chi chuan, meditation, and massage.

Nonwestern communities often have quite different beliefs about what constitutes a mental problem and how to cure it. In traditional healing ceremonies, witch doctors and shamans may perform elaborate rituals in which they appeal to a natural force or to one of the gods.

Shaman
Someone believed to communicate with spirits, usually during a ritual, and who practices healing.

Cross-cultural Psychology

Cross-cultural psychologists study the thought processes, social attitudes, motivations, and beliefs of people in different societies, comparing and contrasting any influences on behavior. Such findings can offer valuable insights into the human mind.

Culture can be defined as the attitudes, values, beliefs, and behaviors shared by a group of people with a common history, which are passed down from generation to generation, principally through language.

As global travel and communication have become common, and a rise in migration has led to increased numbers of people from different cultures living together in a single location, cross-cultural psychology has entered the mainstream of scientific research.

Causes and effects

The main research method cross-cultural psychologists use is called comparative analysis: A researcher obtains data from a sample of people in a particular culture and compares it with other known data or values. A known behavior or value is called a dependent variable: It is an observed, established behavior event or pattern. The researcher is then free to ask which factors might account for the dependent variable and to decide which of these potential causes or

These men of the Dogon people in Mali are wearing elaborate costumes for a ceremony. Cross-cultural psychologists have been fascinated by the similarities and differences between cultures such as this and those of the Western world.

influences to test. These factors are the independent variables in the research study.

Ingroups and outgroups

Social psychologists and sociologists have commonly distinguished between two categories of social groups: ingroups and outgroups. Ingroup relationships are formed with the people we feel closest to and involve various levels of intimacy, trust, or familiarity. Thus a person's ingroups might include family, friends, and work associates. Outgroups are groups to which we feel we don't belong, such as other families, rival sports teams, or different departments at work. There is evidence that ingroup and outgroup relationships in other cultures differ significantly from their equivalents in the Western world.

Individualism and collectivism

Sometimes the theory of individualism–collectivism (IC) is used to explain the cultural differences in ingroup–outgroup relationships. Individualistic (generally Western) cultures are less concerned with people's social responsibilites, encouraging people to achieve power and success in their own right.

Collectivistic cultures tend to emphasize the needs of society as a whole, identifying individuals through their membership in a group rather than their position, rank, or personal qualities. Collectivistic communities also demand greater harmony, cooperation, and cohesion within their ingroups, and individuals are expected to conform and identify with the group.

People in an individualistic society tend to treat outgroup members more equally, making fewer distinctions between their ingroups and outgroups. In collectivistic communities, despite the greater fluidity of roles, people tend to feel aloof and even hostile toward outgroup members.

Individualism–collectivism

A scale that measures how much a particular society promotes individual needs, wishes, desires, and values above group goals.

Curriculum Context

Students should examine how cultural differences can affect personal development in both collectivist and individualist cultures.

Culture-bound illnesses

When psychologists are dealing with behavioral problems, they must look at every aspect of the individual seeking help. Although the main cause of any disturbance is often an unhappy personal history or physical ill-health, culture may also play an important role—and not only may it be partly responsible for the condition itself, but it may also influence the psychologist's response to the illness. Indeed, what is considered normal or abnormal behavior varies considerably from culture to culture.

Research methodology

It is tempting to conclude from this that both the mind itself and the psychological analysis of it may be influenced—and sometimes even governed—by the local culture. However, it is easier to accept this idea than to prove it. One of the problems with culture is that it is a sociological concept, not a biological one, and as such very hard to define. Even if it is agreed that culture is a combination of values, attitudes, behaviors, and beliefs communicated from one generation to another through language and art, this still leaves a huge range of variables that must be measured accurately if they are to be scientifically meaningful.

Sociological
Concerning human society, its structure, and how it functions.

Nevertheless, researchers have shown that these pitfalls can be avoided and have produced valuable information about the psychological significance of various cultural differences. In one study researchers found evidence that human perceptual processes develop differently depending on the particular shapes and angles to which people are exposed daily in their environment. People living in the United States, where many buildings contain 90-degree angles, are susceptible to different optical illusions than people in rural African villages, where structures are more usually curvilinear.

Other cross-cultural studies have led to a reconsideration of older questions, particularly about what constitutes normal human sexuality. Homosexuality, long considered pathological behavior in the United States, is approved of in some cultures, for example, and may even be encouraged as a sexual outlet before entry into heterosexual marriage.

Heterosexual

Concerning attraction between people of the opposite sex.

Cultural Differences

Research carried out in the 1970s by Stanley Sue, a professor at the University of California, appeared to show that psychotherapy was excluding large sections of the U.S. population. Although many North Americans of European descent benefited from analysis, Asian Americans and Native Americans were less likely to seek counseling, and those who did were less likely to find it helpful or even to complete their therapy courses. These results were replicated in a later study in the 1990s, and it was concluded that the problem was caused by the insensitivity of standard treatment methods to the needs of different cultures.

Cross-cultural psychology may also examine the relationship between a dominant culture and any subcultures contained within it. In this instance a subculture is defined as a group of people whose experiences differ from those of the majority culture. A subculture may be constituted in different ways and is often an ethnic, racial, or religious group, although any group that develops its own customs, norms, jargon, and behavior may be so defined, including groups of drug dealers or criminal gangs.

Cross-cultural psychology is a critical field in psychologists' efforts to understand human behavior worldwide. But as we have seen, it is also one of the most difficult fields to study accurately.

Glossary

Aesthetic Concerned with beauty or the appreciation of it.

Agoraphobia Fear of going out in public.

Anatomy The study of the bodily structure of living organisms.

Arbiter Something that settles a dispute or has ultimate authority in a matter.

Articulation The formation of clear and distinct sounds in speech.

Artificial intelligence The science of making machines that can think for themselves.

Assimilate To integrate into something else.

Autopsy An examination of a dead body to discover the cause of death or the extent of disease.

Axiom A statement or proposition accepted as true.

Bile A bitter fluid that is secreted by the liver and aids digestion.

Buddhism An Asian religion founded by Siddartha Gautama in the fifth century B.C.

Buffer In computing, an area of temporary memory.

Classical conditioning Training a person or an animal to behave in a certain way in response to an unrelated stimulus.

Claustrophobic Having an irrational fear of confined places.

Cognitive science Studies of the human mind and how it works.

Cognitive states Mental events relating to thinking.

Correlation The relationship or connection between two or more things.

Cosmos The universe seen as a well-ordered whole.

Cross-cultural Relating to different cultures or comparison between them.

Dyslexia A disorder that involves difficulty in learning to read without affecting general intelligence.

EEG Electroencephalography: the measurement of the brain's electrical activity.

Electrode The conductor through which electricity enters or leaves an object.

Empirical Based on observation or experience rather than on theory or logic.

Epileptic Suffering from epilepsy, a disorder marked by convulsions or periods of loss of consciousness.

Epithumetikon In Ancient Greek philosophy, the seat of appetites and desires.

Evolution The process by which different organisms are thought to have developed, over time, from earlier forms.

Gene A unit of heredity that determines some specific characteristic and that is passed from parent to offspring.

Genetic determinism The idea that behavior is inflexible because it is totally determined by genetic influence.

Genetics The process by which the features of an organism are transmitted to its offspring.

Glucose A sugar that is an important energy source in living organisms.

Hemisphere One of the two halves—left and right—of the brain.

Heredity The passing on of physical or mental characteristics from generation to generation.

Heterosexual Concerning attraction between people of the opposite sex.

Hinduism A major and ancient religion and culture of the Indian subcontinent.

Hippocampus Part of the brain, thought to be the center of emotion, memory, and the autonomic nervous system.

Holistic Characterized by the belief that the parts of something are interconnected and can only be explained by reference to the whole.

Hypotheses (singular: hypothesis) Proposed explanations based on limited evidence and used as the starting points for further investigation.

Hysteria Exaggerated or uncontrollable emotion.

Individualism–collectivism A scale that measures how much a particular society promotes individual needs, wishes, desires, and values above group goals.

Intonation The rise and fall of the voice in speaking.

Introspection The examination of one's own mental and emotional processes.

Larynx The hollow organ holding the vocal cords; the voice box.

Linguist Someone who studies languages and their structure.

Logic Reasoning conducted according to strict rules of validity.

Meditation Focusing one's mind or thinking deeply for a long period for spiritual purposes or for relaxation.

MEG Magnetoencephalography: the measurement of the magnetic fields produced by the brain's electrical activity.

Metabolism The chemical processes within an organism that maintain life.

Methodology The system of methods used in a particular area of study.

Microchip A tiny wafer of semiconducting material used to make an integrated circuit.

Narcissistic Having excessive interest in oneself and one's appearance.

Nativism The belief that mental concepts and structures are present from birth rather than learned later.

Natural selection The process by which organisms that are better suited to their environment are more likely to survive and produce more offspring.

Neurons Brain cells specialized to conduct nerve impulses.

Neuroscience The study of the structure and function of the brain.

Neurosurgery Surgery performed on the brain or spinal cord.

Neurotransmitters The chemicals that transfer impulses from one nerve fiber to another.

Node A point at which several pathways intersect or branch.

Objective Not influenced by personal feelings or opinions.

Obsessive-compulsive behavior Behavior characterized by extreme anxiety and repetitive actions aimed at reducing that anxiety.

Operant conditioning Training a person or an animal to behave in a certain way by punishment or reward.

Parallel processing The ability to carry out several tasks simultaneously.

Pathology Physical or mental disease.

Pathos A quality evoking sadness or pity.

Perception The process by which one becomes aware of external stimuli.

Phenomenon (plural: phenomena) An observable fact, condition, or event.

Phi phenomenon An illusion in which an appearance of movement is created by a series of still images.

Phlegm The secretions of the mucous membranes of the respiratory passages.

Phobias Extreme and irrational fears.

Physiology The study of the way living organisms and their body parts work.

Pragmatism The use that can be made of knowledge and ideas.

Preconscious The part of the mind below the level of consciousness, from which memories and emotions can be recalled.

Psychophysics The application of the principles of physics to mental processes.

Purge Treat by causing vomiting or evacuation of the bowels.

Radio waves A form of electromagnetic radiation that is used for long-distance communication.

Radioactive Emitting ionizing radiation or particles.

Rationality The quality of being based on reason or logic.

Reductionism The practice of breaking behavior down into parts and assuming it is the result of conditioning or physiological drives.

Reflexively Without conscious thought.

Religious order A society of monks, priests, or nuns following particular religious and social disciplines.

Salivate To secrete saliva, a watery liquid that aids chewing, swallowing, and digestion.

Shaman Someone believed to communicate with spirits, usually during a ritual, and who practices healing.

Sociological Concerning human society, its structure, and how it functions.

Subconscious Concerning the part of the mind that influences actions and feelings, but that one is not fully aware of.

Subjective Influenced by personal feelings or opinions.

Survival mechanisms Processes that allow an organism to live through difficult circumstances.

Syntax The arrangement of words and phrases to create sentences.

Theorem A general proposition proved by a chain of reasoning.

Thumos The cause of courage, indignation, anger, and other action-oriented emotional states.

Traumatic Emotionally disturbing or distressing.

Visual cortex The part of the brain dealing with sight.

Voltage difference A difference in electrical potential.

Weaning Moving a baby from breast-feeding or bottle to solid food.

Further Research

BOOKS

Atkinson & Hilgard's Introduction to Psychology (15th edition). Florence, KY: Cengage Learning, 2009.

Cardwell, M. *Dictionary of Psychology*. Chicago, IL: Fitzroy Dearborn Publishers, 2000.

Carter, R. *Mapping the Mind*. Berkeley, CA: University of California Press, 2000.

Dawkins, R. *The Selfish Gene*. New York: Oxford University Press, 2006.

Dennett, D. C. *Darwin's Dangerous Idea: Evolution and the Meanings of Life*. Carmichael, CA: Touchstone Books, 1996.

Eysenck, M., and Keane, M. T. *Cognitive Psychology: A Student's Handbook (6th edition)*. London, UK: Psychology Press, 2010.

Gazzaniga, M. S., Ivry, R. B., and Mangun, G. R. *Cognitive Neuroscience: The Biology of the Mind (2nd edition)*. New York: Norton, 2008.

Harley, T. A. *The Psychology of Language: From Data to Theory (2nd edition)*. Hove, UK: Psychology Press, 2008.

Hayes, N. *Psychology in Perspective (2nd edition)*. New York: Palgrave, 2002.

James, W. *Principles of Psychology*. New York: Cosimo Classics, 2007.

Kalat, J. W. *Biological Psychology (7th edition)*. Belmont, CA: Wadsworth Thomson Learning, 2008.

Kassin, S. M., Fein, S., and Markus, H. R. *Social Psychology (4th edition)*. Florence, KY: Wadsworth Publishing, 2007.

Leahey, T. A. *A History of Psychology: Main Currents in Psychological Thought (6th edition)*. Upper Saddle River, NJ: Prentice Hall, 2003.

McCorduck, P. *Machines Who Think: A Personal Inquiry into the History and Prospects of Artificial Intelligence*. Natick, MA: A. K. Peters, 2004.

Nobus, D. *Jacques Lacan and the Freudian Practice of Psychoanalysis*. Philadelphia, PA: Routledge, 2000.

Owusu-Bempah, K. and Howitt, D. *Psychology Beyond Western Perspectives*. Leicester, UK: British Psychological Society Books, 2000.

Pinel, J. P. J. *Biopsychology (6th edition)*. Boston, MA: Allyn and Bacon, 2007.

Pinker, S. *How the Mind Works*. New York: Norton, 2009.

Ridley, M. *Genome: The Autobiography of a Species in 23 Chapters*. New York: Harper Perennial, 2006.

Rutter, M. *Genes and Behavior: Nature–Nurture Interplay Explained*. Oxford, UK: Wiley-Blackwell, 2006.

Weiten, W. *Psychology: Themes and Variations*. Florence, KY: Wadsworth Publishing, 2010.

Wickens, A. P. *Foundations of Biopsychology (2nd edition)*. Harlow, UK: Prentice Hall, 2005.

Wilson, E. O. *Sociobiology: The New Synthesis*. Cambridge, MA: Harvard University Press, 2000.

INTERNET RESOURCES

American Psychological Association. Here you can follow the development of new ethical guidelines for pscychologists, and find a wealth of other information.
www.apa.org

Association for Behavioral and Cognitive Therapies. An interdisciplinary organization concerned with the application of behavioral and cognitive sciences to the understanding of human behavior.
www.abct.org

Bedlam. The Museum of London's online exhibition about Bedlam, the notorious mental institution.
www.museum-london.org.uk/MOLsite/exhibits/bedlam/f_bed.htm

Exploratorium. Click on "seeing" or "hearing" to check out visual and auditory illusions and other secrets of the mind.
www.exploratorium.edu/exhibits/nf_exhibits.html

Freud and Culture. An online Library of Congress exhibition that examines Sigmund Freud's life and key ideas, as well as his effect on 20th-century thinking.
www.loc.gov/exhibits/freud

Great Ideas in Personality. This website looks at scientific research programs in personality psychology. Pages on attachment theory, basic emotions, behavior genetics, behaviorism, cognitive social theories, and more give concise definitions of terms as well as links to further research on the web.
www.personalityresearch.org

Kismet. Kismet is the MIT's expressive robot, which has perceptual and motor functions tailored to natural human communication channels.
www.ai.mit.edu/projects/humanoid-robotics-group/kismet/kismet.html

Museum of Psychological Instrumentation. Look at images of early psychological laboratory research apparatus.
chss.montclair.edu/psychology/museum/museum.html

Neuroscience Tutorial. The Washington University School of Medicine's online tutorial offers an illustrated guide to the basics of clinical neuroscience, with useful artworks and user-friendly text.
thalamus.wustl.edu/course

Personality Theories. An electronic textbook covering personality theories for undergraduate and graduate courses.
www.ship.edu/~cgboeree/perscontents.html

Seeing, Hearing, and Smelling the World. A downloadable illustrated book dealing with perception from the Howard Hughes Medical Institute.
www.hhmi.org/senses/

Social Psychology Network. One of the largest social psychology databases on the Internet. Within these pages you will find more than 5,000 links to psychology-related resources and research groups, and there is also a useful section on general psychology.
www.socialpsychology.org

Index

Page numbers in *italic* refer to illustrations and captions.

psychoanalysis 13, 38–47,
 53
psychoanalytic theory
 38–39
psycholinguistics 80–85
psychophysics 20, 24
psychophysiology 22, *23*
psychosexual development
 41–42, *41*
Pythagoras 6

R

rasas 99
reaction formation 43
recall tasks 76
recognition tasks 76
reflex arc 30
relational psychoanalysis 46
repression 43
right hemisphere 64
Rogers, Carl 50–52, *51*, 53

S

schema 75
self-concept 50–52
self-psychology 45–46, 50
selfobject 45–46
sensation 24
shamans 101
Simon, Herbert 87
Skinner, B. F. 15, 59–60
SOAR 88
social Darwinism 16
sociobiology 19
Socrates 7
speech segmentation 82
Sperry, Roger 64
Spinoza, Baruch 11
stigmata diaboli 11

strokes 62, 71
structuralism 27, 28, 33
sublimation 43
Sue, Stanley 105
superego 40–41, 42, 43
supervised neural network
 89
Symons, Donald 19
syntax 85

T

Taita people 99–100
Taoism 100–101
therapies
 aversion 61
 behavioral 60–61
 Gestalt 36–37, *37*
 humanistic 36, 51–52
 nonwestern 100–101,
  101
 psychoanalytic 43–45
Thorndike, E. L. 15, 55
thumos 6, 8
Titchener, Edward Bradford
 27
Tooby, John 78
top-down processing 75
Tower of Hanoi 73, *73*
Tukes family 12
Turing, Alan 86

U

unsupervised neural
  network 89

V

visual cortex 68

W

Watson, John B. 15, 56–59
Wernicke, Carl 85
Wertheimer, Max 32–34, *33*,
 35, 36
Williams, George C. 93
Wilson, Edward O. 19
Wilson, Margo 91
witch doctors 101
Wundt, Wilhelm 13, 20, 22,
 24–26, 27

Y

yang 101, *101*
yin 100, *101*
yoga 100
Young, Thomas 20